QUALITATIVE ANALYSIS FOR PLANNING & POLICY

The revised and updated second edition of *Qualitative Analysis for Planning & Policy* is a roadmap to help planners access qualitative data and integrate it into their planning investigations. Planning and policy decisions are not based solely on numbers, and this book equips planners with a how-to guide to see what has been missing "between the lines" of quantitative data and make good decisions using the best possible information.

Each chapter offers step-by-step instruction on how to set up and enact diverse types of qualitative research, and case studies demonstrate how qualitative research techniques can be combined with quantitative methods to tackle complex real-world projects.

For over a decade *Qualitative Analysis for Planning & Policy* has been an indispensable resource for students and researchers, experienced and novice planners. The revised second edition offers myriad tools to help twenty-first-century planners make intelligent decisions, including new qualitative research techniques, technological innovations, and contemporary case studies.

John Gaber AICP is the Department Chair of City Planning and Real Estate Development and City and Regional Planning Professor at Clemson University, USA. Dr. Gaber has over 30 planning research articles published in an assortment of journals including: *Journal of Planning Education and Research, Journal of Architecture and Planning, Evaluation and Program Planning, Journal of Planning Urban Development,* and *Journal of the American Planning Association.* His most recent research projects include: Sherry Arnstein's *Ladder of Citizen Participation,* qualitative research techniques used in citizen participation projects, Hippietowns, and mixed method research strategies.

QUALITATIVE ANALYSIS FOR PLANNING & POLICY

Beyond the Numbers

Second Edition

JOHN GABER

Routledge
Taylor & Francis Group

NEW YORK AND LONDON

Second edition published 2020
by Routledge
52 Vanderbilt Avenue, New York, NY 10017

and by Routledge
2 Park Square, Milton Park, Abingdon, Oxon, OX14 4RN

Routledge is an imprint of the Taylor & Francis Group, an informa business

First edition published by Planners Press Publishing 2007

Library of Congress Cataloging-in-Publication Data
Names: Gaber, John, author.
Title: Qualitative analysis for planning & policy : beyond the
    numbers / John Gaber.
Other titles: Qualitative analysis for planning and policy
Identifiers: LCCN 2019056948 (print) | LCCN 2019056949 (ebook) |
    ISBN 9780367258481 (hardback) | ISBN 9780367258504
    (paperback) | ISBN 9780429290190 (ebook)
Subjects: LCSH: City planning. | Regional planning. | Land
    use—Planning. | Qualitative research.
Classification: LCC HT165.5 .G33 2020 (print) | LCC HT165.5
    (ebook) | DDC 307.1/216—dc23
LC record available at https://lccn.loc.gov/2019056948
LC ebook record available at https://lccn.loc.gov/2019056949

ISBN: 978-0-367-25848-1 (hbk)
ISBN: 978-0-367-25850-4 (pbk)
ISBN: 978-0-429-29019-0 (ebk)

Typeset in Joanna
by Swales & Willis, Exeter, Devon, UK

CONTENTS

TABLES

FIGURES

ACKNOWLEDGEMENTS

This book is the culmination of many years of teaching, research and practice. I want to thank Gordon Scholz at the University of Nebraska-Lincoln, Becki Reztlaff at Auburn University, and my faculty and staff at Clemson University for their ongoing support. To the communities in Alabama, Arkansas, Nebraska, New York, and South Carolina who participated in various planning studies: I appreciate your openness and willingness to tell me what worked and didn't work.

Martin Krieger, Pierre Clavel, and Barry Nocks provided critical feedback at important junctures. Finally, I want to thank my children, Allison, True, Jennifer, Corbin, and Peter for their laughter, patience, and encouragement.

1

INTRODUCTION

THE NEED FOR QUALITATIVE PLANNING RESEARCH

Qualitative research can alter the course of planning in a city. This was the case 25 years ago in New York City. William Whyte's qualitative study of urban spaces in New York helped to redefine the city's zoning code to better accommodate public open spaces. [1] Unfortunately, today's planners are inadequately trained in how to recognize, access, organize, and integrate qualitative observations—which yield data in the form of words and images—into their research projects. This lack of qualitative research skills limits planners to asking questions that can only be answered with quantitative methods, which deal only with numbers. A better knowledge of qualitative research techniques will expand a planner's repertoire of researchable topics beyond what is available through quantitative methods.

This hands-on book for practicing planners, planning students, and planning researchers examines how to use qualitative planning research to see what has been missing "between the lines" of quantitative data. Planning research is only one part of the range of influences (zoning codes, city ordinances, comprehensive plans, and politics, for example) that go into making a plan. Planners are already well-versed in quantitative research methods as prescribed by the American Institute of Certified Planners exam, Planning Accreditation Board for American planning schools, and existing planning research methods books. But as evidenced by William Whyte, planners cannot afford to ignore qualitative research strategies when they are confronted with nonquantifiable problems.

Planners do research when they need more data to make intelligent decisions and know that planning decisions are not based solely on the numbers. Because qualitative research is often deemed too costly in terms of time or money, planning researchers are not well trained in qualitative research strategies. They commonly mistake qualitative data as either politics, "common sense," "street smarts," or worse yet, file them away as outside the purview of the research project, never allowing their observational insights to make a significant impact in the planning process. Many times, planners cannot see the qualitative data through the lines of previously generated quantitative data. This book is a road map to help planners access qualitative data and integrate them into their planning investigations.

To respond to the oft-cited criticism that qualitative research is too resource-intensive, I offer the old adage: Pay now or pay later. A classic example is the large-scale public housing projects built in the 1950s and 1960s. Professionals now widely recognize that these projects were a bad idea. However, at the time, the quantitative planning research pointed toward high rates of poverty and the high cost of housing. The housing projects were seen as the solution: Move thousands of low-income residents into huge, high-density residential facilities that can accommodate thousands of individuals (but which, as we know now, show little consideration for basic community life needs).

The Pruitt-Igoe housing project in St. Louis had to be demolished because it did not work for its residents, even though it had won an AIA (American Institute of Architects) design award. If a qualitative inquiry had been done beforehand, the planners would have found that socially isolated, high-density residential dwelling units for low-income families did not produce a positive neighborhood environment. In this classic example, the expense of a qualitative research strategy at the onset could have potentially saved millions of dollars in housing projects and spared thousands of low-income residents from being trapped in socially isolated towers in the park.

To better acquaint planning researchers with qualitative research methods and data, I first look at the overall research process or "research act." [2] The first section of this introductory chapter discusses the research process, which includes data steps, how to develop a researchable question, how data relate to research methods, how to choose a method, and how to know whether the data are valid and reliable. The second section provides an overview of the organization of the book. Here, I briefly discuss the focus of the remaining chapters and explain how they come together to form a planner's approach to qualitative research. Throughout the book, I provide real planning applications and examples.

DATA STEPS

The foundation of planning research is the "research act," [3] the process of constructing research activities. The research act is divided into five sequential steps in relation to data: Establishing the question (need for data); accessing data (methodology); organizing and analyzing data for its observations of reality (analysis); testing the significance and reliability of data (confidence and reliability); and presenting the research results.

An example of a planner in a mid-sized southern city shows how these research activities work in concert. The planner is interested in changing a two-way street in the industrial section of town to a one-way street to better accommodate large trucks and their deliveries to local area businesses, but is confronted with a series of questions and needs data to answer them. The first step in the research act is establishing the research question. One of the questions is: What do local business owners think about this proposal? Having established this research question, the planner then moves on to the second step in the research process and chooses a survey methodology to access the data about what the business owners think. The planner drafts a survey, asks that peers and superiors provide input, then mails the survey to the businesses immediately impacted by the proposed one-way street.

After a month of receiving completed surveys, the planner moves on to the third step in the investigation—organizing and analyzing the data. Here, the researcher inputs all the survey responses into a spreadsheet, then analyzes the data to see how the survey data speak to the larger issue of changing the two-way street to a one-way street to better accommodate truck traffic. In analyzing the data, the planner learns that local business owners support having a one-way street, but are concerned that modifications made to the street would hamper public access to their buildings. After the analysis is complete, the planner goes to the fourth step in the research process and tests the significance, validity, and reliability of the data to check on its veracity. At this point the planner checks the validity of the observations ("Am I drawing the right conclusions about the data?") and the reliability of the research method ("Did my survey instrument work properly?").

Once confident that the observations are accurate and that the research instrument was reliable, the planning researcher moves on to the last step. The research project concludes when the planner reports and presents the research findings to planning colleagues so results can be integrated in the final planning proposal. The research was successful in determining the business owners' perspective and in providing insights on how the changes to the street should consider customer access to the businesses. There will be more to this analysis later.

DEVELOPING A RESEARCHABLE QUESTION

The quality of a researchable question is based on its ability to guide the planning researcher to efficiently obtain needed data. According to Patrick White in his book *Developing Research Questions* (2009), good researchable questions have four key parts: (1) Clear picture of needed answer, (2) accurate location of needed data ("population of interest"), (3) good understanding of research variables, and (4) realistic assessment of the research project. (See Figure 1.1.) All investigations begin with a simple question: "what do I need to know to be able to make an informed planning or policy decision?" As obvious as it sounds, "if you do not know exactly what kind of evidence is required by your research question, you will be unable to choose the most appropriate research design and methods of data collection and analysis." [4] Knowing what answer you are looking for does not mean you know which direction your data will point to during the data analysis stage of the investigation. For example, in a transit-oriented development research project where a community housing planner is searching for the answer to the question; "where are people coming from to access the local subway stop?", she does not know where people are coming from at the start of her research project.

It is important to know the location of your needed data. Data are everywhere and include people, buildings, images, research reports, artifacts, and meeting transcripts that can be found in multiple locations. There will most likely be several different locations/sources that will have part or all of your data. For example, in the City of Greenville, South Carolina, open space data (undeveloped land) can be found in the Departments of Community Development, GIS, Parks

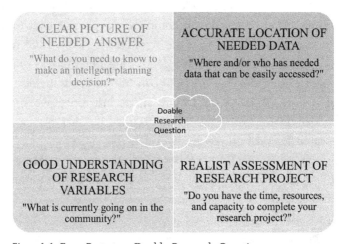

Figure 1.1 Four Parts to a Doable Research Question

and Recreation, Parking, Planning and Zoning, and Public Works. Part of the function of research methods is to help you locate data that you need to answer your research question.

In developing your research question, the more you know about what is going on in the community, the more precisely you will be able to identify key issues (variables) that are impacting the community. For example, a community development planner needing information on how she can develop more housing opportunities for low- and moderate-income families will first need to have a basic land use understanding on the location of low- and moderate-income neighborhoods, schools, primary employers, public infrastructure, parks, and existing zoned land uses.

Planners and policy makers conduct applied research projects that commonly operate within tight time constraints and on limited budgets. "The time and money you have at your disposal will have fundamental implications for the kind of research questions that you can realistically address." [5] You need to make sure that the research question you ask can be answered with a research technique that fits your timeframe and budget. Some research techniques can take months to complete (e.g. focus group investigations) while other techniques can be completed in an afternoon (e.g. photographic research).

Of the five steps in the research act, the most significant is determining what type of research methodology (methods to access data) is needed to answer the question. Asking the right question, but accessing the wrong data, leads to, at best, partially answered questions; at worst, inconclusive data.

To understand why accessing methods are important, you first need to understand data. Sidestepping the philosophical debate of empirical reality, in this book I assume that researchable reality is multifaceted and complex. Some parts of reality can be understood as being governed by laws. For example, Isaac Newton's law of gravity illustrates an understanding that gravity controls everything on earth: What goes up must come down. This "Newtonian" understanding of reality supports traditional scientific quantitative research. Other parts of reality are not governed by laws but are constituted in relationships and experiences. John Dewey's "experiential" understanding supports a more exploratory and naturalistic approach to research.

Empirical reality is not static or single-faceted. Instead, we better understand it as dynamic with a kaleidoscope of characteristics. As planning researchers, we cannot understand all of the reality on a particular topic. But we can, with the right research method, collect data providing a very good image of some of the reality we are studying. A clear distinction exists between reality and data.

RESEARCH METHODOLOGY

One way to visually illustrate empirical reality in relation to data is to imagine reality as a multifaceted cake and research methods as techniques that take observational slices out of the empirical cake in the form of data. Data give planning researchers insight into what reality is all about. In fact, I like to think of data as "data slices." [6] (See Figure 1.2.)

Each data slice we take out of the empirical cake gives us one particular insight into reality. The type of methods we use to generate data slices determines what we know about empirical reality. The complex characteristics of reality can be loosely organized into the two types of data I discussed earlier: Quantitative and qualitative. Quantitative data require research methods that are good at capturing data on shared population characteristics and general patterns for an entire community. [7] (Qualitative data require research methods that allow the researcher to ask exploratory and descriptive questions. (See Table 1.1 for a detailed distinction between the two data sets.). Qualitative data fit in the "experiential" understanding of data.

To illustrate how different questions are more in tune with different slices of data, look at the differences in the questions two community planning research approaches ask. A quantitative research approach asks questions to access numeric data sets that work well with a more precise research technique. For example,

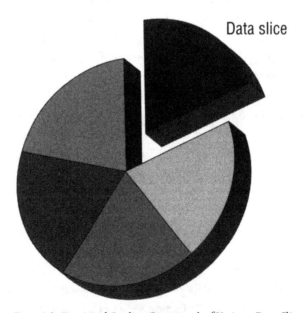

Figure 1.2 Empirical Reality Composed of Various Data Slices

Table 1.1 Distinguishing Characteristics between Quantitative and Qualitative Data

Quantitative	Qualitative
Positivist in orientation, seeking objective facts about and causes of social phenomena with little or no reference to subjective states of individuals	Phenomenological in orientation, seeking to understand human behavior from the social actor's own frame of reference
Obtrusive and controlled measurement	Naturalistic and uncontrolled observation
Objective	Subjective
Removed from the data: The "outsider" perspective	Close to the data: The "insider" perspective
Verification-oriented, inferential, confirmatory, and hypothesis-testing	Discovery-oriented, descriptive, exploratory, inductive
Outcome-oriented	Process-oriented
Reliable; "hard" and replicable data	Valid, "real," "rich," and "deep" data
Generalizable; multiple case studies	Tends to be ungeneralizable; single case studies
Particularistic	Holistic
Assumes a stable reality	Assumes a dynamic reality

how many people live in the community? What is the demographic profile of the community, such as the number of unemployed and youth? How have these numbers changed over time? All of these questions look at the external characteristics of the empirical cake. How tall is the cake? How wide is the cake? How much does the cake weigh? These data slices give precise quantitative insights about the cake but tell us nothing on what is going on inside the cake.

A qualitative research approach will ask less precise research questions and more accurate questions that focus on process and how things work on the inside. For example, how do members of the community spend their free time? How do low-income residents make ends meet? How does race impact where people live and send their kids to school? Quantitative research questions look at the internal characteristics of the cake. What type of cake is inside? Is it marbled? If so, what is it marbled with? Does the type of icing work well with the cake? This type of data slice provides a more accurate qualitative insight about what is going on inside the cake but provides us with little precision about its size or dimensions.

In this book I take a "paradigm of choice" approach to research methods, which means, essentially, "different methods are appropriate for different situations." [8] This leads us to two assumptions about research methods themselves. First, all research methods are techniques that help planning investigators access data. No one research method stands out as technically better than another. The second assumption advances that some research methods better access certain data slices than other methods, that qualitative methods (for example, focus group research) are technically better at accessing qualitative data slices than quantitative methods (for example, census data analysis), and vice versa. Accepting these assumptions gives you, as a researcher, the choice to do a quantitative investigation, qualitative investigation, or a mixture of both (mixed method research investigation) based on the needs of the research project, rather than catering to popularly held professional perceptions of what constitutes "solid research" (which is usually quantitative research).

This approach puts the research question and data in the driver's seat in determining the direction of the research project. Such an approach is contrary to a mono-method research strategy where the planner accesses only quantitative or qualitative data. In a mono-method approach, you must modify your question to fit your particular data slice strength. This approach puts research method ahead of the research question and the needed data sets. In this scenario, you might find yourself researching only those topics for which particular research techniques can access data.

Thus, the most important research decision you'll make is choosing the method best suited to access data. The next section examines this very central concern.

CHOOSING A QUALITATIVE METHOD

After establishing the research question, ask yourself: Is this information already available? The most common mistake new planners make is being too eager to develop original research on planning problems. Before you take on a new research project, first quickly exhaust simple, easy, and accessible data slices (completed office research reports, sister agency reports, government documents, and Internet resources). Given the tight timeframe within which the plan-making process works, you might sometimes find it better to get quick, easy, and dependable research results from past studies that closely approximate the problem at hand, rather than redirect scarce resources to a new research project that, at best, marginally adds new observations, or, at worst, duplicates past research findings.

How can you decide if original research is needed until you know what data slices you'll need and find out if they're already available? If someone has already conducted research that addresses the same question you need to answer, then no new research is needed. If there is a gap in past research, new research is needed to answer the question. For example, I worked on a research project that analyzed nonfuel purchasing patterns of truckers at truck stops in 2001. In 2006, we got an e-mail from a researcher thanking us for our research because they were asking the same question as in our 2001 research report and now did not have to conduct the research themselves.

If original research is needed, you'll move on to the next question: What type of data slice do I need—quantitative or qualitative? If the research question is about park use and the data to be collected are the number of people who use the park, the question "How many children use the playground equipment?" requires a quantitative approach. But a question about how the park works, such as "How do the children use the playground equipment?," requires a qualitative approach. To answer this question, find out what type of "use" data the planning director, city council, or neighborhood residents expect to learn. Sometimes research questions can read very similarly (How is a park used?), but empirically ask very different questions. Visualize the type of data you need to answer the research question. By understanding how the data may look (process versus magnitude) you'll be able to better choose which research method you need to access these data.

Qualitative data have six characteristics that make them attractive to planning researchers. These six traits can be used together as a diagnostic tool to help you determine if you need to access qualitative data. (See Table 1.2.)

You should have the research question at hand to see if the data slice needed fits any one or all of these six qualitative data characteristics. First, qualitative data provide a view into human events and activities in their *natural settings*. This naturalistic perspective yields observations "on selves, social objects, rules of conduct,

Table 1.2 Prominent Qualitative Data Characteristics

Trait	Application
1. Natural Settings	Capturing the ebb-and-flow of everyday life
2. Context	Getting the big picture
3. Process	Finding the connective tissue that tie a series of events together
4. Description	Documenting the finer details of what is going on
5. Unanticipated Discoveries	Discovering situations that defy quantification
6. Community Involvement	Bridging the gap between planning researcher and the community they plan with

social situations, and social relationships." [9] Here, qualitative data allow you to take the subject's perspective on a particular situation. For example, how a person sees a community center while driving past at 35 miles per hour is different from how a person sees the same community center when she is standing in front of it. The second characteristic, context, is also known as the holistic approach. Qualitative data adhere to the understanding that the economy, social structure, environment, and politics are all interrelated parts making up a community. This approach focuses on what is happening in terms of the entire community. Qualitative data provides images of entire neighborhoods and communities.

Closely associated with context is the process characteristic of qualitative data. Embedded in qualitative data is the understanding that everyday life is a stream or process, interconnected to different events. The process part of qualitative data looks at structured activities that move people within events, as well as move people between events. Allan Jacobs' 1980 documentation of the San Francisco planning process, especially for the Transamerica Building, and his height and bulk zoning ordinance case studies, illustrate good examples of qualitative data capturing the various influences affecting the flow of life within these planning events. [10]

Description—more specifically "thick description" according to anthropologists—is widely accepted as the backbone of qualitative data. [11] The more finely detailed the description, the higher the confidence of the qualitative data. A fine description of a particular neighborhood shows the planner took the time and effort to learn something about the area. Thick description proves to local community members that the planner can be trusted to know the subject. A thick description of a situation investigates motives, context, and popular explanations for specific events.

In the months I spent researching street vendors on 14th Street in Manhattan, I learned the phrase "knowing what time it is" had a special meaning to the local vendors and had nothing to do with time. To "know what time it is" on 14th Street meant the person knows all the activities taking place on the street, with a particular awareness of the location of all police officers. This kind of in-depth detail gave my data credibility among street vendors and with local policy makers.

Qualitative data also observe and capture activities not easily quantifiable through unanticipated discoveries. They bring to the forefront situations that no one knew existed. The informal economy and illegal activities are two examples. One illustrative example is how New York City planners discovered the idea of converting manufacturing lofts in SoHo and Greenwich Village to residential use. A New York City planning staff member told me this story. City officials were trying to figure out what to do with the glut of turn-of-the-century manufacturing lofts in the southern midsection of Manhattan. It was looking into the costly idea of demolishing the outdated buildings to make way for much-needed commercial and residential land uses. One weekend, a New York City planning staff member, walking among the lofts in Greenwich Village, discovered a banana peel in the gutter and fresh residential garbage in the dumpster on the sidewalk. Finding this curious, he revisited the area several times over the next few days to discover that people, mostly artists, were illegally living in the lofts. This discovery, combined with Sharon Zukin's research on loft living [12], led to New York City's planning for residential loft conversion.

Finally, community involvement places the planner directly in the environment she studies. To access qualitative data, she goes out to the site, interacts with the community, and experiences what life is like with people who live in the community. Qualitative research moves away from removed "armchair research" of secondary data and forces planning researchers to get involved with real people in real situations. [13]

Qualitative research techniques facilitate community involvement in the research stage of the plan-making process in two ways. First, by forcing the planner to leave her office and interact with members of the community, qualitative research data (for example, field research or focus groups) allow the planner to become acquainted with the data on a first-name basis. Second, qualitative research allows the converse: The community gets involved in the research process by talking with the planner. By talking with people in the community, the planner hears stories about daily events and the effects of these events on the residents. The interpersonal interactions between the planner and the community allow the community to make sure the planner obtains all the necessary data slices to reach the best possible understanding of the situation at hand. This type of data gathering commonly happens in focus group research. People in the community go out of their way to make sure that the focus group facilitator gets a clear picture "from my point of view."

QUESTIONS OF VALIDITY AND RELIABILITY

For all methodological tools, questions of validity ask whether or not a data slice gives the correct portrayal of reality. Both quantitative and qualitative data are vulnerable to challenges of validity and reliability. Questions of internal validity ask if the researcher made the correct observation based on the available data. However, unlike quantitative data, qualitative data lack the statistical tests (for example, t-test or chi square) that better protect the researcher from questions of internal validity. This makes it more complicated to defend qualitative research results. Most questions of internal validity for qualitative research focus on possible researcher bias and any distortion or obfuscation of the observations.

Researcher bias can distort your observations in four ways. First, the researcher's personal characteristics may predispose her to working more closely with certain types of informants while giving short attention to, or outright ignoring, other informants. As a result, she captures only part of the story. It purports to portray the "big picture" although it is actually biased toward one point of view.

A transit research project I participated with in Jamaica, Queens, New York, showed this distortion. With the help of a handful of graduate planning students from Columbia University, we interviewed early-morning subway riders standing on the platform to find out how they got to the station (walk, taxi, bus, friend drove them) and why they were taking the subway into Manhattan. The interviewers found that most people waiting on the platform were not going to work, but rather going to school, shopping, or a doctor's appointment. This seemed odd to us, so I started looking more closely at the data and found that almost three-quarters of the interviewed respondents were between the ages of 18 and 30. We saw then that the student surveyors, all single men going to graduate school, had a proclivity to interviewing persons in their age group, thus biasing the results of the interview. Discovering this researcher bias, we had to hire additional women investigators to the research team and retrain the male investigators and return to the subway platform to increase the number of older interview respondents. Needless to say, our research findings dramatically changed.

Second, the researcher's personal, philosophical, and theoretical beliefs may bias the execution of the research technique enough to affect the study's final results. The researcher in this case has her mind already made up about the direction of the research project, about which members of the community are important sources of data, and about which other members of the community are less important.

I experienced an example of this bias when I was sitting in on the final presentation of a homelessness study in Nebraska being conducted by a private planning consulting firm. One of the key questions was: What caused homelessness in Nebraska? The firm conducted a series of focus groups with staff from homeless shelter providers to access these data. At the end of the presentation, I asked the planning consultant if he conducted any focus group meetings or personal interviews with homeless people to poll their views on what caused their predicament. The senior planning researcher for the study confidently stepped to the microphone and said, "Homeless people do not know what causes homelessness, so we did not talk to them." The researcher in this study clearly had his mind made up about homeless people and his particular biases were showing up in the study. To him, the homeless people were the problem, not the community needing assistance.

Third, the terms used by the researcher may bias their research findings and have confused community members who were accessed for the study. This check on validity is called "construct validity" and focuses on how "terms, generalizations, and meanings are shared across time, settings and populations." [14] This is a vexing problem in planning research because planners use a wide range of acronyms (CBD, PUD, EIS, GIS), awkward phrasing (pedestrian friendly transit), and multisyllabic words (urban regeneration) that can be misunderstood as a foreign language to everyday citizens. It is easy to see how community members participating in a focus group research project would be intimidated and confused if the planning researcher began the session by saying: "I am looking at a pedestrian friendly PUD urban regeneration development project in the CBD that is part of mix-method GIS study that is required by a local mandated EIS." The key here is to ground the construct of key terms in your study to a literature that is widely recognized by professionals in your field and are clearly translated to everyday terms that everyone (professionals and locals) agree on.

The last, and more common, form of researcher bias happens when the investigator "goes native." Here, the researcher adopts the position and perspective of the community she is studying, sometimes at the expense of her allegiance to the government, nonprofit, or funding client who is paying her to do the study. This obligation can be challenging. Nothing captures the essence of "going native" better than Elliot Leibow (who is white) and his study of African American "streetcorner" men in a low-income community in Washington, DC, in the 1960s:

I am not certain, but I have a hunch that they were more continuously aware of the color difference than I was. When four of us sat around a kitchen table, for example, I saw three Negroes; each of them saw two Negroes and a white man. [15]

In the social sciences, researchers are discouraged from this type of investigation because it is almost impossible for an "outsider" to be accepted as an "insider." If a researcher does get accepted as a member of the community, her exit plans to leave the community at a specific point in the study significantly decrease the likelihood that she was ever truly native in the first place. In planning, unlike the pure social sciences, going somewhat native is actually encouraged. We call it "advocacy planning." [16] Planners who are members of a neighborhood (for example, a historic district) or active members in a community (for example, a Native American planner living on a reservation) can provide valuable "native" perspectives to a planning investigation. The dilemma is, however, that while professionally it is more accepted for the researcher to adopt the position of disadvantaged populations and environments, she is not free to forsake the ethical responsibility of carrying out methodologically defendable research projects, simply because she takes an advocate's position. The best way to conduct powerful advocacy planning research involves the planner clearly stating her focus before the study is executed, minimizing this question of internal validity.

Questions of external validity focus on how far a planning researcher can generalize observations of a particular research project to other related situations. Since qualitative research generates a tremendous amount of data in the form of "thick description," its empirical observations generated from one qualitative research project are not transferable to other research projects simply because the two case studies have different social, economic, political, cultural, and environmental factors. For example, we cannot compare detailed observations about morning rush hour traffic in New York City with morning rush hour traffic in Los Angeles. Most Los Angeles commuters live and work in Los Angeles County and drive to their destinations. In New York City, a large number of the commuters come from outside the city itself, and even New York County and New York State, and many take subway or commuter trains. At this level of analysis, this is an example of comparing apples to oranges.

This is not to say that qualitative research results cannot theoretically inform other similar situations. "Theoretical inference" is possible when planning researchers draw big-picture conclusions from one qualitative research project and apply them in another. [17] Going back to the Los Angeles-New York City commuter example, the two cases do have some shared characteristics. During rush hour, both cities have large numbers of people going to work and school at roughly the same time. Comparing rush hour traffic at a larger scale in these two different cities is defensible to the issue of external validity. The question for theoretical inference is: At what level can observations be transferred? That answer can only be determined on a case-by-case basis.

The question of reliability looks at the consistency of the research technique. Does it regularly produce the same result, regardless of the topic it is analyzing? The primary interest here is the replicability of the research technique. For example, a hammer will hit a nail in the same way as it hits your thumb. What the hammer hits (the results) does not change how the hammer strikes the target. But reliability in a research technique does not equal validity. For example, a thermometer may consistently get the same reading of body temperature, but may be getting the reading consistently wrong. In this case the thermometer is reliable; it gets the same reading over time. But it is not valid, because it consistently gets the wrong body temperature.

On the other hand, the validity of a research project is greatly substantiated with reliable research techniques. Going back to the thermometer example, a highly precise digital thermometer provides more confidence in recording body temperature than a classic mercury thermometer. Since qualitative research lacks the precision of quantitative research, the reliability of qualitative research is slightly compromised by its very nature. Yin [18] provides excellent advice for qualitative planning researchers addressing the question of reliability in their investigations: "The general way of approaching the reliability problem is to make as many steps as operational as possible and to conduct research as if someone were always looking over your shoulder." When doing qualitative research, make sure another planning investigator, using the same technique, could get the same data.

HOW THIS BOOK IS ORGANIZED

This book is composed of seven chapters, each divided into three sections. Four chapters look at specific qualitative research techniques: Field Research (Chapter 2); Photographic Research (Chapter 3); Focus Group Research (Chapter 4); Content Analysis and Meta-Analysis (Chapter 5). The last two chapters discuss the application of qualitative research techniques within a larger "big picture" mixed method research project (Chapter 6) and for the purpose of citizen participation applications (Chapter 7).

Field research allows planning researchers to go out into the community and systematically observe an event or check the status of a current situation. Three types of field research strategies (nonparticipant observations, participant observations, and full participant observations) are discussed in this chapter. The range of data slices obtained from field research techniques varies from simply counting trucks parked at a rest area to assessing subtle changes in a revitalized commercial corridor.

Next, I discuss the empirical approach to photographic research. Planners have been obtaining and using visual images in their reports for illustrative purposes (for example, a picture of rush hour traffic in Los Angeles) for decades. In this chapter, I move the use of images from that of illustrations ("This is a picture of ...")

to empirical data ("This image provides new insight into our research question in the following ways …").

Focus group research is commonly used in planning investigations, but it is unfortunately commonly botched largely because the researchers have a hard time figuring out what to do with the spoken comments they collect. In this chapter, I discuss how to set up a focus group meeting and provide hands-on meeting facilitator advice as well as how to organize and analyze verbal data.

Content analysis and meta-analysis are strategies that look at secondary data sources (for example, newspaper articles and research reports) to develop large-scale observations on the current thinking about a particular situation. Content analysis is used to analyze verbal text data generated in focus group and established research investigations. It has been extensively used in research on homelessness to help planners generate a big picture understanding of the NIMBY (Not-In-My-Back-Yard) responses of communities fighting the location of homeless shelters in their neighborhoods. Meta-analysis is a recent extension of content analysis. This is an investigative technique where the planner is able to collectively look at several different research publications and analyze them as one large "meta" pool of data.

At the beginning of each research technique chapter, I define the research method and discuss the most common reasons to use this research technique. Next, I provide an overview of the technique and how to apply it in an everyday research situation. After discussing the ins and outs of the technique, I discuss how the method relates to questions of internal and external validity and reliability. Two actual case studies are then provided to show how a particular research technique is used to analyze a real problem (for example, how I used field research to examine truck parking at interstate rest areas) with real applied planning consequences. At the end of each chapter, I connect the reviewed research method to current technological tools.

Chapter 6, "Getting the Big Picture," takes a detailed look at mixed method research strategies. Mixed method investigations are those that combine qualitative data slices with quantitative data slices into a single research project. This multimethod research strategy is well established among evaluation researchers, whose job it is to assess the effectiveness of social, health, and education programs. They have been extensively using mixed method research investigations for over 30 years and the technique is now making inroads with planning practitioners. In this chapter, I outline the most commonly used mixed method strategies and provide an overview on how the qualitative techniques discussed in this book can work into mixed method research projects.

The last chapter looks at qualitative research techniques commonly used by planners in their citizen participation projects. The community-based nature of qualitative research techniques makes them useful tools for planners to systematically engage targeted segments of the community and provide alternative ways to record and analyze their lived experiences. Three qualitative research techniques (walking interviews, stakeholder and key informant investigations, and Photovoice) that are widely used in citizen participation projects are reviewed in this chapter.

Cumulatively, this book offers experienced and novice planners alike three contributions to expand their cadre of research techniques: (1) How to use qualitative methods, (2) how to innovate and update these methods, and (3) how to integrate these methods with more "traditional" quantitative methods.

As more planners have questions that can be answered through qualitative research strategies, we will start seeing problems in a new dimension, which may in turn bring about new ways of solving them. The profound relationship of method to solution is captured in Umberto Eco's observation: "It is through method that (we) arrive at the solution." [19]

DISCUSSION QUESTIONS

1. The type of questions you ask can play a critical role in dictating the type of conclusions you make in your planning investigation. Pick a specific planning issue (e.g. access to sidewalks in North Charleston, South Carolina, to increase physical exercise as a way to combat obesity) and ask the same question (what is the need for more sidewalks?) but in the two different approaches to data: Quantitative and qualitative. How does the type of approach to data change the nature of the research question? Do different approaches to data result in different types of observations generated in the research project (depth versus precision)? Are there situations where quantitative and qualitative oriented questions can generate the same overall observations?

2. Questions of external and internal validity of a planning research project is context specific. Pick a planning research topic that focuses on answering internal and external validity questions to a very local case (e.g. urban revitalization of the Collier Heights neighborhood in Atlanta, Georgia). Recalibrate the scope of your research topic so it addresses questions to internal and external validity to a much larger community (e.g. community development in Atlanta). How did the research project change in the two different investigations in terms of methods used in each study? Why is it valid for you to apply the findings from the larger study (City of Atlanta) to better understand a local problem (Collier Heights), but not valid to apply the findings from the local study to the larger audience? How can you readjust your research conclusion from the local study to make them applicable to the larger study?

3. Different approaches to data can yield the exact same observations. Many times as a planner researcher you will need to get creative and figure out how to get data on a particular community issue that are not easy or cost effective to obtain with the most direct research approach. Pick a specific planning issue (e.g. needs of the transit disadvantaged in the small Nebraska town of Wahoo) and design two different research projects (quantitative and qualitative) that can get at the same community observations.

REFERENCES

[1] Whyte, W.H. 1988. *City: Rediscovering the Center*. New York: Anchor Books.

[2] Denzin, N. 1989. *The Research Act: A Theoretical Introduction to Sociological Method* (3rd ed.). Englewood Cliffs, NJ: Prentice Hall.

[3] Denzin, *Research Act*.

[4] White, P. 2009. *Developing Research Questions: A Guide for Social Scientists*. New York: Palgrave Macmillan, p. 90.

[5] White, *Developing Research Questions*, p. 77.

[6] Glaser, B., and Strauss, A. 1970. "Theoretical sampling," in *Sociological Methods*, edited by N. Denzin. New York: McGraw-Hill, p. 108.

[7] Sayer, A. 1992. *Method in Social Science* (2nd ed.). London: Routledge, pp. 242 and 244.

[8] Patton, M. 1988. *Qualitative Evaluation Methods*. Beverly Hills, CA: Sage, p. 19.

[9] Denzin, *Research Act*, p. 71.

[10] Jacobs, A. 1980. *Making City Planning Work*. Chicago, IL: Planners Press.

[11] Geertz, C. 1983. "Toward an interpretative theory of culture," in *Contemporary Field Research*, edited by R. Emerson. Prospect Heights, IL: Waveland Press, p. 55.

[12] Zukin, S. 1989. *Loft Living: Culture and Capital in Urban Change*. New Brunswick, NJ: Rutgers University Press.

[13] Feagin, J., Orum, A., and Sjoberg, G. 1991. "Conclusion: The present crisis in U.S. Sociology," in *A Case for the Case Study*, edited by J.R. Feagin, A.M. Orum, and G. Sjoberg. Chapel Hill, NC: The University of North Carolina Press, p. 272.

[14] LeCompte, M.D., and Goetz, J.P. 1982. "Problems of reliability and validity in ethnographic research," *Review of Educational Research*, 52(1), pp. 31–60, p. 53.

[15] Leibow, E. 1967. *Tally's Corner: A Study of Streetcorner Men*. Boston, MA: Little, Brown & Co, p. 248.

[16] Davidoff, P. 1965. "Advocacy and pluralism in planning," *Journal of the American Planning Association*, 31(4), pp. 331–338.

[17] Hammersley, M. 1992. *What's Wrong with Ethnography?* London: Routledge Press, p. 91.

[18] Yin, R. 1994. *Case Study Research: Design and Methods* (2nd ed.). Thousand Oaks, CA: Sage, p. 37.

[19] Eco, U. 1989. *Foucault's Pendulum*. New York: Ballantine Books, p. 384.

2

FIELD RESEARCH

WHAT IS FIELD RESEARCH?

Field research is the process of learning about a community, neighborhood, or environs through first-hand observations. Field research requires the investigator to have a purposeful strategy before going out to the study site. It is common practice for the planner to systematically record insights and observations in field notes.

WHY DO PLANNERS NEED FIELD RESEARCH?

You will need to conduct field research when you do not have access to enough data about a particular community, place, or activity in order to make an informed planning decision. Planners choose field research strategies to obtain data that are context-specific. This method assumes that the specific problems planners research are embedded in a larger system of "interrelated parts," [1] and that by researching the larger context, the planner gains a better understanding of the problem. The researcher tries to capture a holistic, "big-picture" perspective that integrates what people say and do within the context of larger social, economic, physical, environmental, and political factors.

Field research investigations can obtain both quantitative and qualitative data slices. An example of quantitative field research would be a manual vehicle count to determine traffic flow; qualitative research would generate thick descriptions of what drivers did when they got stuck in traffic. Cost is another reason for field research. Sometimes it is easier, less expensive, and less time-consuming for a planner to get first-hand observations than to apply other research approaches.

Research strategies like focus groups, surveys, and photographic research require more time to set up and implement and some investment in equipment, while field research can be as simple as a planner visiting the research site a handful of times, sitting on a park bench, and witnessing life unfolding before her very eyes. Herbert Gans describes the simplicity of field research like this: "It takes time, some paper, pencils, and shoe leather, but if necessary, it can be done by one person—without a research grant." [2]

Finally, field research gives a planner an effective way to incorporate the community's perspective in the plan-making process. At times, planning research can be an extremely insular practice. With research strategies like GIS (Geographic Information System), the planner can consider herself an expert on a community and never have stepped foot in it. A planner chooses field research when she wants to personally connect with the community and learn what its members are experiencing at their place and time. It is a research method that assumes John Dewey's "immediate empiricism," considering the community itself as a valuable source of empirical data. [3] By understanding what the community is experiencing on an immediate level, the planner can better integrate its perspective into the research phase of planning.

DOING FIELD RESEARCH

Field research strategies are commonly divided into three types: non-participant observation, participant observation, and full participant observation. Non-participant observation describes when the planner is physically present at the research site, or in the community, but she purposefully does not participate in the activity happening there. She is there simply to observe. The most common non-participant observation strategies used in planning research are windshield surveys, site reconnaissance, and complete observations.

Participant observation occurs when the planner either participates or interacts with the community as a planning researcher. The planner can develop relationships with members of the community, but it is a planner–community relationship. The most common participant observation research strategies are structured or semistructured field interviews and unstructured observations.

Full participation occurs when the planner drops her professional identity and strives to be accepted into the community as a full-fledged member. After spending time in the community, she returns to her professional role to report on her experiences. This "going native" research strategy is extremely rare for planners—even for sociologists and anthropologists—and is subject to much methodological debate about the validity of observations generated from it.

Each of these types of field research strategies comes with its own research perspective and levels of obtrusiveness and analysis (see Table 2.1). Research perspective identifies whose perspective the data reflects. Field research strategies can provide observations from either the planner's point of view ("This is what I see") or can strive to give the views of the community ("This is what the community is experiencing"). Obtrusiveness deals with how involved (or how in the way) the planner is with the community and the local environment when she is making her observations. The higher the planner's obtrusiveness in the field research strategy, the greater the risk of questions about internal validity and researcher bias.

The level of analysis identifies the geographic scale a particular field research strategy can best handle, given its methodological limitations. As seen in Table 2.1, the larger the scale of observation, the less obtrusive is the strategy (and the lower the risk of researcher bias). However, the community's perspective is lost.

Table 2.1 Type of Field Research Strategies

	Type of Field Research Strategy	Research Perspective	Obtrusiveness	Level of Analysis
Nonparticipation Observation	a. Windshield Surveys	Distant, researcher perspective	Little	Regions, cities, neighborhoods
	b. Site Reconnaissance	Distant, researcher perspective	Little	Communities, neighborhoods
	c. Complete Observation	Distant, researcher perspective; some community awareness	Some	Neighborhoods, blocks, parks
Participant Observation	a. Structural/ Semistructured Interviews	Less distant, researcher perspective; more community awareness	Some/More	Communities, neighborhoods, blocks, parks
	b. Unstructured Observations	Community perspective	More	Communities, neighborhoods, blocks, parks
	c. Full Participation	Community perspective	Most	Communities, neighborhoods, blocks, parks

NON-PARTICIPANT OBSERVATION

Windshield Survey and Site Reconnaissance

Both windshield survey research and site reconnaissance investigations take the same experiential approach to field research, albeit at different scales. In a windshield survey, you will visually examine a large area while riding in a car or bus. [4] Observations generated during the survey are your impressions of the context and conditions of the research site. If you are using a vehicle, it is best to have at least two people to conduct this investigation so one person can drive while the other person observes and records what they see. An example of a windshield survey is a planner researching a central business district in relation to the surrounding low-density suburbs.

A site reconnaissance investigation entails a planner walking several blocks in a neighborhood, business district, or park, and recording first-hand impressions. This technique provides the planner with an "opportunity to experience the quality of life in the area" [5] to discover its most significant aspects. The planner walking a handful of blocks in the CBD and briefly talking with local shop owners is an example of site reconnaissance.

Setting Up

Before beginning a windshield survey or site reconnaissance, you will need to organize your travel logistics and figure out what to look for. You will choose the research site within a neighborhood, community, city, or regional context and document the route you anticipate taking during your expedition. The path and direction you identify in the mapping section of your field research are dictated by the research question at hand: What data do you need from the field? (In all field research expeditions, opportunities often present themselves that lead you away from the expected path. Side trips are encouraged in this line of field research. Sometimes they expose you to an entirely different understanding of the community than you were initially exploring.)

After figuring out where to go, you will need to identify a schedule of when to go and at what time. Often, the time, day, and season determine what you see. By systematically identifying where, how, and when you plan to do your windshield survey or site reconnaissance prior to entering the field, you will have a more efficient process of obtaining observations, as well as a better comparison of different legs of the expedition.

Finally, you need to know what you're looking at. This requires you to do your homework about the research site and its region: Its location on a map, secondary descriptive information (census statistics, topographical data), history, and such. Getting preliminary information about the research site and region allows you to develop a loose list of topics (variables) for which to look. Listing the anticipated variables allows you to compare different legs of the trip to each other and to do a cross-comparison of the observations of different field investigations. In the example of a windshield investigation looking at the relationship of a CBD to the surrounding suburbs, the research focus may be oriented toward public recreational facilities. While out in the field, the planner will pay particular attention to the public parks and recreation areas in the two areas.

Getting the Data

You can record your windshield survey and site reconnaissance data in several ways. [6] (Windshield survey investigations will gather more macro-level observations which are better recorded with written or oral impressions, visual documentation (photographed or hand drawn), detailed maps with annotations, or tabulations (counts of off-ramps, dwellings, factories).

You will use roughly the same processes to record site reconnaissance observations (for example, photographs), but your observations will be much more detailed because they cover a much smaller research site. Your detailed observations (for example, overhearing local catchphrases spoken in the cafés) and recorded artifacts make site reconnaissance research particularly powerful since the details prove to the community that you took the time and effort to carefully learn about the research site.

Organizing the Data

The observations made from a windshield survey and the observations and artifacts (physical pieces of evidence such as an announcement for an upcoming neighborhood meeting obtained while walking the research site) gathered during site reconnaissance explorations are all connected to the geographic locations where they were discovered. As a result, you must geo-reference each observation, artifact, map, drawing, or photograph to the location where you experienced or found it. After completing your expeditions, you can organize your recordings and artifacts in one of two fashions: (1) Assembling the materials as chapters in a journey, documenting the many features of the region or research site, or (2) organizing all the materials into a comprehensive collage of what was experienced in the field.

Analyzing the Data

The analysis of data collected during a windshield survey or site reconnaissance usually falls into one of three (or a combination thereof) empirical observations: significance; trends and themes; and discrepancies. Since both of the field research approaches depend on your "impressions," the significance of windshield survey and site reconnaissance data is the degree of impact the field experience had on you as a planner. Here, you need to comb through your recordings and artifacts and assess the magnitude of what you observed in the field (for example, a severe degree of poverty, wealthy suburban residential developments, or deteriorating old industrial factories). Second, you need to look for consistent trends or themes. Are the same experiences regularly recorded at the same locations? (For example, have you consistently recorded several abandoned homes in the same residential development?) Analyzing data for consistent observational themes allows you to evaluate field research data for discrepancies among observations. When you look for differences between your observations, you are making a closer investigation of situations that do not conform with your overall observations of the area and trying to figure out why they are different.

For example, you might observe more abandoned small commercial buildings in the older, southern part of town than in the newer, northern part of town. Upon closer investigation of the southern part, you learn that one of the reasons why commercial retail is in decline is because a new regional shopping center recently opened a few miles away that has proven to be too much competition for local retailers.

Complete Observation

When you need to get observations by isolating and analyzing a few identifiable variables, you will probably use complete observation field research strategies to place you physically at the research site or event without interacting with the participants or the environment. You hope to minimize researcher bias by removing yourself from interacting with the observable variables. The best planning example of this type of research is William Whyte's study of downtown public open spaces in his book *City, Rediscovering the Center*. Whyte describes his full observation method like this:

> ... we watched people. We tried to do it unobtrusively and only rarely did we affect what we were studying. We were strongly motivated not to. Certain kinds of street people get violent if they think they are being spied upon. [7]

Examples of complete observation field research investigations can be as large-scale as an analysis of bison use of groomed roads in Yellowstone National Park, to as small-scale as William Whyte's records of pedestrian movement and activities on two blocks of Lexington Avenue in Manhattan. [8]

Setting Up

Before you start obtaining field research data, you need to answer two questions. First, what are the variables that will be observed and recorded in the investigation? Research variables include areas of inquiry planners want to learn more about—events, people, activities, animals, and such—anything that can be observed or heard in the field. Identifying observable and recordable research variables is rarely rocket science and usually very matter-of-fact. William Whyte describes it like this: "For the past 16 years I have been walking the streets and public spaces of the city and watching how people use them." [9]

After identifying what to observe in the field, you ask the second question: "What are the relationships among the identified variables?" By already picking the research variables to be observed, you have implicitly assumed a tentative theoretical connection among or between them. Answering this question requires you to explicitly state what you think the relationship may be among the research variables. I am not recommending that you ascribe to a formal hypothesis statement that identifies a positive relationship between two or more variables, where the manipulation of one variable (independent variable) causes a change in another variable (dependent variable). Instead, I suggest that you take a more "interactive" interpretation between identifiable variables.

Explaining the relationship between research variables and why they are important is determined by the literature on the subject matter. [10] (In transportation planning, for example, the literature on estimating trip generation from a residential area looks at a series of variables (household income, number of persons in the household, number of vehicles owned by the household, and population density) that should be considered in the study.) [11] Research in this field has found that the number of vehicle trips has a positive relationship with household income, number of persons in the household, and number of vehicles owned.

Getting the Data

Several issues need to be addressed before actually going out into the field. First, what kind of data will you record? Usually, this becomes fairly obvious after you describe the relationship between the identified research variables. Second, and closely connected to the first, is the question of the quantity of data you need to get. The answer is largely a function of two factors. The first is how much time you have to conduct the study. Planning research always operates within artificial time constraints. Planners rarely get enough time to do all the research they feel necessary. So, the amount of data you collect from full observation research is dictated by the time available, along with other obligations, scheduled deadlines, or how much of the grant is budgeted for field research.

The second factor is how close you are to reaching the point of *saturation of observations* in the field research project. Saturation occurs when you are not learning anything new and the cost and effort of going out into the field outweighs the benefits of additional field observations. Saturation of observation signals that the full observation leg of the research project is at an end.

Next, think about the tools you need to record your observations; full observation research can be extremely data-intensive. The most common instruments used to record field observations are still and video cameras, frequency measuring devices (for example, traffic counters), clipboards, and pencils.

The last issue that you need to think about is the viewpoint from which you will take your observations. It is important to eliminate research bias by decreasing your influence on field activity. Thus, you should take extra measures to decide how you will observe the field without being detected. For example, you might observe pedestrian flow on a sidewalk by sitting by a window in a café.

Organizing the Data

You will organize your observations based on how the field research data are recorded. Most commonly, the data are organized according to one or a combination of three ways: statistical frequency, mapping, and detailed descriptions. Statistical frequency analysis is the most common. Standardizing the observed research variables allows you to compare the field observation of one site to observations taken at other sites. Mapping allows you to show your full observations on a map or an image of the research site. These field observations are usually shown either as types of activities (for example, talking, eating, or sitting) or as frequency of activities (the number of times people stop and talk, eat, or sit) at the research site.

Your write up will discuss some of your finer-grade observations in detailed descriptions. The goal is to provide the reader with a sense of what life is really like out in the field. Although these descriptions never give the full sense of what the community experiences, they can produce an excellent descriptive context showing the community at a particular time. If done correctly, detailed descriptions paint images that mentally transport the reader to the rhythm and flow of the research site.

Analyzing the Data

The analysis of full observation projects studies what was or was not found in the relationships among research variables in the field. You may find an observable relationship, no relationship, or unanticipated relationships. When doing full observation field research, you always hope you will actually observe relationships among the identified research variables. The analysis here, however, is less a celebration that a relationship was found ("We were right!"), and more a documentation, a measurement of magnitude, and a discussion of some of the more subtle characteristics of the relationships. Sometimes anticipated relationships among research variables never materialize. As in true science, the failure to prove a relationship among variables does not necessarily mean a failure in the research project. Many times these non-relationships between variables help you realize that things may not be as simple as they appear. Finally, there are times when you will anticipate one set of outcomes between variables, but come up with a different and more insightful analysis instead. These new discoveries provide you with a better concept of what is really going on in the field.

Physical Trace Measures

Physical trace measures is the most detailed and most unobtrusive field research technique. This is when you look at physical evidence "specifically produced for the purpose of comparison or inference that was the result of past behavior." [12] Physical evidence data can be as obvious as a 70 foot alleyway over-filled with used bubble gum stuck to the walls in San Luis Obispo, California, to as faint as finding a couple dozen hypodermic needles in Zuccotti Park, New York City. Trace measure research can be divided into two broad classes of evidence: erosion measures or accretion measures. [12] When the planning investigator is searching for erosion physical evidence, she is looking at the purposeful selective wear on materials (e.g. the wearing-away of hospital floor tiles as evidence of heavier foot traffic) to illustrate past activity. In accretion physical evidence research, the community health investigator looks for materials left behind (e.g. beer bottles in a neighborhood park parking lot) to document past behavior and estimate the people who were involved in the activity.

Setting Up

You need to have a clear idea where you are going to obtain your observations when conducting trace analysis. This does not presuppose that you already know what you will find at the research site. In most trace analysis research projects, the planning investigator does not know exactly what they will find. You are a detective in search of clues about a research site and how it is connected to other activities and events. Knowing that trace analysis only focuses on recording evidence from past events and activities, you need to schedule your research site at "off-times" so you do not influence the flow of activities that leaves traces at your research site. For example, if you anticipate a public open space is being used for unsanctioned skateboarding, you showing-up to the open space with a camera when skateboarders normally skate will most likely deter them from skating in the open space.

Getting the Data

The research tools used for trace analysis will be similar to complete observation research; still and/or video camera and field notebook. Contrary to complete observation research that strives for a saturation of observations, in trace analysis you only need to record an example of evidence of past activity and are not required to record the full extensiveness of the past activity. For example, in documenting skateboarders using park benches for their tricks, you only need to document evidence from one park bench instead of documenting all the park benches used by the skateboarders.

Organizing the Data

How you organize your physical trace data depends on which class of evidence (erosion or accretion) is being obtained. In erosion trace analysis you need to be able to depict the depth/volume of the activity being documented. This is usually captured with photographic images and requires you to depict the image of the activity you are documenting in relation to an easily understood object to illustrate magnitude. For example, Figure 2.1 is a trace analysis of flooding in Nichols, SC, produced by 2018 Hurricane Florence. In this image, notice the height of the flooding from the watermark on the white shutters in relation to the front door of the house.

Figure 2.1 Flooding in Nichols, SC, as the Result of Hurricane Florence

Analyzing the Data

Physical trace analysis is being able to depict the physical trace of an object (image of a flooded house) and provide the explanatory connection on why the object is significant in the community. One example of accretion physical trace research is Jason Corburn analyzing local knowledge in the combating of asthma in the predominately Hispanic community of El Puente in the south side of Williamsburg, Brooklyn, in New York City. "New York City has one of the highest rates of asthma in the United States." [13] Rates of asthma are particularly high among Latino and African-American children in the city and it has hit the El Puente community very hard. Corburn uses physical trace analysis and looks at street art to learn more on what the community is thinking about childhood asthma. Below he describes an extensively drawn mural by the students from the El Puente Academy.

> *The mural covers the exposed wall of a three-story corner building in the heart of the community. It depicts some of the triggers of asthma (e.g., air pollution and cockroaches), what happens to the body during an asthma attack (e.g., red, inflamed lungs) and what suffers can do for treatment (e.g., using inhalers, and women making herbal remedies). [13] (See Figure 2.2.)*

Figure 2.2 El Puente Asthma Mural
(Jason Corburn, Street Science: Community Knowledge and Environmental Health Justice. Cambridge, MA: MIT Press, 2005)

PARTICIPANT OBSERVATION

Structured and Semistructured Interviews

For both types of interviews, you will go out to the community and directly ask local residents questions that relate to the research project. Structured interviews require you to closely follow the interview guide, but you have more leeway in semistructured formats. For example, you might change the order of questions asked in the field or ask follow-up questions to the interviewee after she provides an interesting insight.

Setting Up

The best type of interview format is determined by what you want out of the research. There are strengths and weaknesses associated with both structured and semistructured interviews depending on whether you are looking for speed, sample size or depth, or detailed answers. (See Table 2.2.) If you are interested in interviewing a large sample of the population but less interested in detailed answers, look more to a structured interview. If you are less interested in getting a representative sample, are dealing with a smaller community, or are

Table 2.2 Criteria for Determining Structured Versus Semistructured Field Interviews

	Structured Interviews	Semistructured Interviews
Speed	Faster: Structured format allows the planner to ask more questions in less time. More interviews can be completed in a shorter time than in semistructured interviews.	Slower: Looser structure allows for more time to talk between questions. Semistructured interviews will take more time to complete than structured interviews.
Sample Size	Larger: Questions in a structured interview tend to be more focused, allowing the interviews to be conducted in a more efficient fashion.	Smaller: Given the conversational openness of semistructured interviews, they take more time to implement. Semistructured interviews do better with smaller samples or when community representation is less important.
Depth	Less: More inclined toward closed-ended and short questions. Structured interview responses tend to be shorter and have fewer community stories than semistructured interviews.	More: Questions are embedded in a conversation, allowing for more detailed responses. Much more likely to have open-ended questions and long and detailed responses.

interested in more detailed answers, choose a semistructured interview format. An example of structural interviews that was conducted with a very large interview population was conducted by Bailie et al. in their investigation of housing-related factors affecting child health among indigenous Australian communities. Out of 326 eligible households in the Northern Territory (NT), they interviewed 285 houses that had children (covering 618 children in total) paying particular attention to three factors in their interviews: (1) Overcrowding, (2) quality of house infrastructure, and (3) hygienic condition of the houses. [14] They concluded that documenting housing improvements did not directly translate to improvements in the health of individual children. [15] Instead, improvements in children's health need to combine specific home infrastructure improvements with concurrent hygiene improvement programs aimed at the broader community.

Once you finalize the interview format, think about how you plan to do the interviews in the field. "Getting in" to conduct field interviews is much easier than getting in to conduct participant and full participant observations. Usually it will be enough to offer prior notification to local authorities informing them of the research project and who will be interviewed. Many times in field interview investigations, the professional visual cues—employee badge, clipboard, government or corporate shirt or uniform, government vehicle—not only frame the social interaction between you and the community residents, but also collectively provide you with a "visa" for recognition, acceptance, and integration into the community.

Field interviews are organized around easily understood researcher roles; you ask a series of questions. Your intentions are made obvious to everyone interviewed by the type of questions that you ask in the meeting.

In a participant or full participant observation project, the researcher's role is more ambiguous; you are watching and talking with people in a particular setting. Your motives are less clear to community members because they never really know what you are looking for or recording.

Getting the Data

Now you need to figure out how to easily record the interviews and retrieve them later. You can record field interviews either by hand on an interview form or through audio recordings. Manually recording responses on an interview form is useful when you intend to interview large numbers of people or if the observations are short and closed-ended, or both. Audio or video recordings of individual comments are more useful when there are fewer people to interview and when the interviewees are answering open-ended questions that allow them to explain their observations.

Organizing the Data

Field interview data organization is very straightforward because the investigation is largely organized around the interview guide questions. At this stage of the research project, you will tabulate closed-ended responses and record open-ended comments. The easiest way to do this is in a spreadsheet. This also allows for easy data retrieval, making it easier to code interview responses in the data analysis section of the research project.

Analyzing the Data

Interview data analysis ranges from a quantitative analysis of a large sample of structured interviews made up of only closed-ended questions to a qualitative analysis and a careful reading of what a few people said in a series of open-ended interviews. When analyzing closed-ended questions, you will look at the statistical distribution of the answers, such as the number of people (broken down by demographic cohorts) who felt public safety was the most important factor in renovating an urban corridor. One benefit of analyzing responses to closed-ended questions is the development of statistical analysis of these observations, a task usually less labor-intensive than analyzing responses to open-ended questions, especially when the data have been put into a spreadsheet.

On the other side of the spectrum, you will look at more intricate details of individual comments in the interviews as you analyze the answers to open-ended questions. For example, one person may comment that she did not feel safe walking down a particular urban corridor at night because there is not enough lighting and there are too many high bushes around the buildings where potential attackers can hide.

Unstructured Observations

In unstructured observational research, you enter the field armed only with a critical eye, an open ear, and motivation to learn from the community. Commonly known as "ethnographic field research," in this line of investigation you regularly visit the research site to develop first-hand familiarity with the community and how it operates on typical and atypical days. As you revisit the research site on a routine basis, local residents will recognize you as a "visiting" member of the community. It is important to note here that the community recognizes you as an outsider—the "researcher" participating in the community—and not as a member of the community. Through recognition, acceptance, and hopefully, integration, you will be able to access people, events, and experiences that are not possible to access through other research strategies. In addition to getting data that is not easily obtained through conventional research methods, ethnographic investigations strive to learn the "community's perspective" in the field.

Setting Up

Starting an ethnographic field investigation is similar to starting a windshield survey or site reconnaissance research project; you physically go out to get first-hand data from the research site. Ethnographic field research differs from other investigations in that it requires you to visit the same research site repeatedly in order to get fine-grain observations.

After defining the research questions, you must decide your vista of observations and what is going to be recorded. The vista of observations not only determines what you will see and experience, but also whose community perspective you will record. The location determines what type of data you will record. As with windshield survey and site reconnaissance research strategies, you will need to map out the research site to determine the best place to start the research. Within the process of determining the research site, you will decide if you are going to be stationary (sitting on a park bench) or mobile (walking or driving round the community). Of course, a stationary research approach requires a much smaller research site than a mobile research approach, which can cover anything from a few blocks to several miles.

The openness of ethnographic field research can make recording your observations a bit overwhelming. Before going out, decide what you will spend most of your time doing. Will you spend most of your time actively talking with local residents or take a more passive role and simply "hang out" with folks in the community and listen (more than talk) to local conversations? Practically speaking, ethnographic research is never just talking or just watching. It usually is a mixture. However, before you go into the field, you will make a decision on what type of primary observations (stories, experiences, and such) to take from the field.

Getting the Data

For most seasoned field researchers, the hardest part of ethnographic research is "getting in" the field to get the data. What makes getting in so difficult is that the planner's role as the researcher is a very obscure concept for the general public. "Tell me again why you are standing on the street corner watching people walking on the sidewalk?" is a common reaction. Each field research project presents you with its own unique circumstances, forcing you to devise a specialized strategy on "packaging" yourself to the public. Come up with a one-sentence explanation about your field activities, something like, "I am standing on the street corner watching the use of the sidewalk because I am interested in learning how people use the public benches." To help ease the transition, try to connect with known "gatekeepers" in the community, such as local shop owners. Gatekeepers, also known as the unofficial "mayors" of the community, are people whom everyone knows and who know everyone. Gatekeepers can help get the word out about what you are doing in the neighborhood.

After you're initially accepted into the community, you will work on maintaining existing relationships and striving to develop new ones. The more people you know, the more perspectives you will get, which expands the breadth of experiences you see, hear, and witness. You will have to reintroduce yourself to new contacts and renegotiate relationships with existing contacts to gain access to more complex and less obvious data slices. By your regular visits, people in the community will learn that you are committed to learning from them.

Distinguishing exactly what data are sometimes presents a special challenge. A good rule of thumb is to keep watching and listening for data along four general parameters: [16] Setting (the research site itself and its relationship to neighboring areas), actors (the populations or people most important to research project), events (activities that are important to the research project), and process (documentation of the evolving flow of events and actors, within the setting).

So, when you know where to look (setting), who to watch (actors), and what activities are the most important (events), you will have a good handle on the type of field data to capture when they present themselves. For example, if you are conducting research to analyze how people use public street furniture, you will choose settings that have public street furniture, watch actors that use (not just sit on) the furniture, and observe the process of how people approach, use, and depart from the public furniture.

Organizing the Data

Everything you see, hear, and experience is recorded in your field notes. These notes are the basic tools that all ethnographic researchers use to transfer discordant field experiences to analytical data. It is standard research protocol for the planner to record each foray into the field within the first day or so to ensure that the finer details of the experience are recorded. Anything and everything should be recorded and stored in field notes. This information includes images, recordings, videos, drawings, figures, tables, letters, objects found in the street, interview data, and personal assessments.

Because ethnographic investigations are so open, field notes should be organized into distinct categories to allow for the efficient retrieval and analysis of the data. Shatzman and Strauss [17] provide an easy "three package" model for organization: Observational Notes, Theoretical Notes, and Methodological Notes.

Your observational notes are recorded accounts of what you saw, heard, experienced, or witnessed. They are meant to be factual observations of what happened, with no deliberate interpretations. Theoretical notes are where you identify ideas, interpretations, or reflections. You record your observations about the research process itself in the methodological notes, which tend to be personal diagnostic observations on what worked and what did not work in the field. In addition to organizing your field notes according to the Shatzman and Strauss model, you should earmark each field recording with the date, time, weather if applicable, and location of the visit.

Analyzing the Data

Making sense out of ethnographic data can be an extremely complicated task for the simple reason that ethnographic research combines a disparate range of data slices, including casual conversations, witnessed events, and everyday experiences. Before you can analyze the ethnographic data, you must first organize the data by coding key words, phrases, events, names, and locations that have any relevance to the research question. Coding field notes gives an immediate gauge of significance, including what was recorded several times and what was recorded less often. Once you have finished coding, you then analyze the data, ferreting out significant observations from less significant ones. Usually (though not always), the substantive topics coded the most frequently will be the more significant topics in the ethnographic analysis. Once a hierarchy of significant observations is determined, you should look for links between significant observations, then try to connect significant observations to less significant ones. In analyzing the linking relationships between coded variables, look for influencing relationships (x influences y) or contextual relationships (x and y are commonly seen together) among units of observations. It is through the linking of coded variables that you can piece together the "big picture" of what is going on in the community.

Full Participation

Full participation field research is not a common strategy in planning, for two reasons. First, it is very hard for outsiders to be accepted in closed communities. Second, full participation requires a tremendous amount of the researcher's time. However, some precedent exists for full participation field research among advocacy planners in the form of community-based research. Here, advocacy planners living among or closely with a particular community can provide a special inside perspective. Instead of going into the community to conduct full participation research, advocacy planners come out of these communities and provide observations based on their lived experiences. One example of this application is Sharon Zukin's research on New York City loft conversions recorded in her book, Loft Living, which is based on her personal experiences as a "loft dweller" beginning in 1975 in Greenwich Village. [18]

QUESTIONS OF INTERNAL AND EXTERNAL VALIDITY AND ISSUES OF RELIABILITY IN FIELD RESEARCH

Questions of internal and external validity and reliability are the Achilles Heel of all field research investigations. Unlike in physics, for example, where a scientist can show the math to prove that a formula is correct, the planner using field research strategies has little to show outside of artifacts, field notes, and images to prove the accuracy of the observations. Proving that your field data are correct depends on your thick description and your ability to explain how and why things work in the community. Given your limited repertoire of methodological tests to prove the validity of your findings, take extra care in anticipating these questions before, during, and after you conduct your field investigations.

Internal Validity

The questions of internal validity you may need to address vary depending on which type of field research strategy you have applied in your investigation. The four most common challenges are whether your obtrusiveness influenced a community's comments and activities; whether or not you incorrectly interpreted what was recorded in the field; whether or not you obtained a representative sample of the community; and whether there was data bias resulting in people in the community acting and stating things that were not representative of their true state of affairs.

Table 2.3 shows how the four field research strategies compare to the four most common questions of internal validity used to judge field research investigations.

The most common solutions planners use to combat questions of internal validity are mixed method research, multiple researchers, and field cross-validation (see Table 2.4). Combining field research with other research strategies in a mixed method approach can shore up some of the limitations inherent in field investigations. For example, survey research can be combined with complete observations or unstructured ethnographic observations to both expand the sample size of the number of people contacted in the research and to provide a cross check to test for bias in the field data. Involving more than one researcher in the investigation opens up several options to the field research project by expanding its geographic range and sample size; deploying researchers with different individual characteristics helps protect against researcher obtrusiveness and data bias. In addition, using more than one researcher to read field observations helps protect against questions of wrongful data interpretation.

Table 2.3 Most Common Questions of Internal Validity in Field Research Investigations

| | | Type of Field Research | | | |
		Windshield/Site Reconnaissance	Complete Observation	Interviews	Unstructured Observations
Type of Question	Obtrusiveness	People change behavior once observed by the planner	People change behavior once observed by the planner	People said what they thought the planner wanted to hear	People change behavior once observed by the planner
	Interpretation	Only saw and/or understood part of the big picture	What was recorded was accurate, but the explanation of what was observed was wrong	Incorrect reading of the interview data	Planner misunderstood what people said and did
	Sampling	Not a representative sample of the community	Planner missed the big picture, or the other side of the story	Not a representative sample of the community	Not a representative sample of the community
	Data Bias	Community prepared for the visit and put on a good face	People acted as they thought they should	People lied	People lied and acted as they thought they should

External Validity

It's very easy to avoid questions of external validity, which focus on observations generalized to apply outside the research area. Remember that all field investigators can generalize their observations only within the territory where their observations were taken. With one exception (described below), field observations cannot be applied to different situations, no matter how similar they appear. Applying them to alternative situations would fail the question of external validity.

Specific field observations can be raised to a higher theoretical level when they are framed as general characteristics rather than specific functions. The one exception to the question of external validity is this: Observations made from one case study can be applied to another when the observations are made at a

Table 2.4 Solutions to Combat Questions of Internal Validity in Field Investigations

| | | Common Questions of Internal Validity | | | |
		Obtrusiveness	Interpretation	Sampling	Data Bias
Solutions to Address Internal Validity	**Mixed Method**	Using different methods to access different data to check on the obtrusiveness of the researcher	Using different methods to access different data to help explain field observations	Using different methods to access different data to access more members of the community	Using different methods to access different data to cross-validate field observations
	Multiple Researchers	Some researchers may be perceived as less obtrusive than others	Using multiple researchers in the field to rule out bias of interpretation with one researcher analyzing the data	Multiple researchers can cover more territory in the field	Multiple researchers can cross-validate what different people said
	Cross-Validation	The researcher can test how obtrusive her presence is in the field by talking with other members in the community.	Not applicable	Not applicable	Getting a different perspective from different members of the community

theoretical level. A traffic research example illustrates this point. A Los Angeles traffic planner analyzing factors that contribute to traffic congestion notices that traffic accidents on Interstate 405 tend to cause traffic congestion. Immediately after an accident, drivers coming up to the accident site tend to slow down to gawk at the accident, causing even more traffic. Even drivers on the other side of the freeway going in the opposite direction, who are in no way impacted by the traffic accident itself, slow down to survey it.

How Los Angeles commuters adapt to the traffic accident site (honking, hand signaling, yelling to cars merging into a different lane to avoid the accident site) is particular to Los Angeles commuters and is not transitive to Chicago, Miami, or New York traffic accident situations. But the general human tendency to gawk at traffic accidents, causing additional traffic, is theoretically transitive to other traffic analyses.

Reliability

The issue of reliability is tricky. Reliability in research methods equates to confidence that different researchers using the same research method in the same location would roughly generate the same observations as the original planner in the initial investigation. On the one hand, in most of the field research strategies discussed in this chapter—windshield survey, site reconnaissance, full observation, and field interviews—you want the confidence associated with the reliability of the research strategy. Thus, when you use any of these field research methods you should strive to make all the steps in your investigation extremely transparent to make sure the project's reliability is not questioned. The community will see that the observations generated in the investigation were not the result of chance or special circumstance that would prevent the research project from being replicated by a different researcher.

On the other hand, a certain "pioneer" element is associated with field research projects, giving you some leeway in field investigations. When you go into the field, you have the opportunity to take advantage of impromptu opportunities where you gain access to small "jewels" of data—you may witness a special event, share in a private conversation, or work on a community project. These are impossible to capture with less flexible field research strategies, such as structured field interviews. You will have some leeway resulting from your unique characteristics as the researcher and the project's organization, which will allow you to be less constrained by concerns of reliability or replicability. However, field research's loose adherence to concerns of reliability makes it that much more vulnerable to questions of external validity because the case study is unique.

CASE STUDY #1[1]: SITE RECONNAISSANCE: NORTH 27TH STREET MULTIETHNIC ENCLAVE

Field research can be simple: You go directly to the research site and start making observations. This is what commonly happens with site reconnaissance investigations. In this case study, I discuss the application of site reconnaissance to get a quick understanding of an emerging multiethnic enclave on North 27th Street in Lincoln, Nebraska. This investigation not only confirmed the existence of several ethnic enterprises, but also clarified the diversity of countries represented in the mix of businesses creating a unique multiethnic marketplace.

By far the most significant reason for Lincoln's growing multiethnic community is the large influx of refugees to Nebraska starting in the mid-1980s. Lincoln, located in the heart of the Great Plains, is not commonly thought of as a hotbed of refugee in-migration. Statistically, the number of resettled refugees in Nebraska is not very remarkable in comparison to other states. For example, the number of refugees that resettled in the state of California between 1983 and 2000 is more than the number of refugees that collectively resettled in all of Colorado, Kansas, Montana, Nebraska, New Mexico, North Dakota, Oklahoma, South Dakota, Texas, and Wyoming during the same time.

What makes the Lincoln case unique is that, from 1997 to 2000, more than 80 percent of all refugees who moved to Nebraska settled there. This is contrary to national trends that indicate refugees tend to resettle in the state's largest metropolitan areas. In 2000, Omaha, with a metropolitan population of 390,007, resettled only 9 percent (55) of the state's refugees, while Lincoln, with a 2000 metropolitan population of 225,581, resettled 91 percent (501).

As part of an ongoing research project, I speculated that a Vietnamese ethnic enclave was developing on North 27th Street. An ethnic enclave is the spatial clustering of co-ethnic businesses, such as the Cuban immigrants who co-located their businesses in "Little Havana" in Miami. [19] Between 1983 and 2000, refugees from 32 different countries of origin were resettled in Nebraska. Of these, 38 percent were from Vietnam; 13 percent from the former USSR; 12 percent were Vietnamese Amerasian; 10 percent were from Iraq; 10 percent came from the former Yugoslavia; and 17 percent were from the remaining 28 countries.

Three distinct geographic characteristics accompany ethnic enclaves: (1) Proximity to ethnic customers, (2) proximity to coethnic businesses, and (3) proximity to a coethnic labor market. [20] I was able to access spatial data from a local nonprofit organization that identified where refugees were relocated in Lincoln. Inputting this data in a GIS analysis, I found that 85 percent of all refugees initially relocated in Lincoln are concentrated in a 4-square-mile downtown area within a city that is over 76 square miles in size. Roughly 41 percent of refugees resettled along North 27th Street.

At first glance, the street appears to be a handful of "Chinese" restaurants. In working with a group of students, we applied a simple site reconnaissance research strategy to get more fine-grain detail and learn more about what was actually happening there. What we learned forced us to rethink our earlier understanding of North 27th Street and the ethnic enclave theory. We created two research teams, each with two graduate planning students, to walk down both sides of the street. The students mapped out each business on every block of the street, recorded the type of businesses, and, if it appeared to be an ethnic business (for example, a Vietnamese video store), recorded which country of origin the store seemed to be representing. In addition to documenting the businesses, the students were told they could go inside to look around and talk to the owners if they felt comfortable doing so.

The research documented 30 ethnic businesses on North 27th Street, strategically located next to each other and within easy walking distance to their coethnic customers. (See Figure 2.3.) Most of the business owners interviewed said they located there because it was where most of their ethnic customers live, confirming our hunch about the development of an ethnic enclave because of the recent refugee resettlement in the area. What we did not expect to find there was the development of a multiethnic economic enclave with several ethnicities represented. This is in contrast to the well-established monoethnic economic enclave described in the literature, such as Koreans in "Koreatown" in Los Angeles. [21] Of the 30 North 27th Street businesses, half were Vietnamese-owned and included restaurants, a pool hall, nail salons, a law office, doctors' offices, a jewelry store, a clothier, retailers, a deli/grocery store, and a video store. Another 25 percent of the businesses were owned by Spanish-speaking refugees and immigrants, while the final 25 percent were owned by Middle Eastern entrepreneurs.

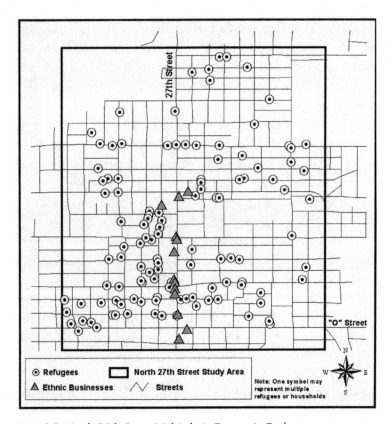

Figure 2.3 North 27th Street Multiethnic Economic Enclave

The discovery of a multiethnic economic enclave in Lincoln establishes a new way to think about ethnic economic enclaves and provides a unique multicultural economic resource to the city. What happened as a result of this site reconnaissance research is a new awareness of a vibrant international marketplace in the heart of Lincoln. This discovery has opened up a new experience for long-time Nebraska residents who are now coming in contact with people, tastes, and cultures from around the world. Lincoln is now working on creating a zoning overlay for the North 27th Street area, establishing it as an international ethnic marketplace both to protect existing businesses and to try to attract more ethnic businesses.

CASE STUDY #2": FULL OBSERVATION: NEBRASKA COMMERCIAL TRUCK PARKING ANALYSIS

This case study provides a classic example of how quantitative data can produce a *precise* understanding about a particular situation but fail to generate an *accurate* understanding of what is actually going on in the community. The most common, and probably the most powerful, reason why planners select field research is to learn directly by entering the community to collect context-specific data slices. This case study is an illustration from a group research project that integrated a full observation field research investigation with a federally mandated quantitative supply and demand analysis for the state of Nebraska. By being open to integrating qualitative research into a quantitative study, the client (the state) received a much more complex understanding of the supply, demand, and actual use of truck stop and rest area parking in the state than what the federal government originally wanted to know. It is this more "holistic" understanding of Nebraska truck parking that is helping state truck parking officials to start planning new rest areas and redesigning older rest areas to meet a growing demand.

The Federal Highway Administration (FHWA) required all states to determine if there was a shortage of commercial vehicle parking and to identify ways to reduce identified shortages. In 2000, the Nebraska Department of Roads (NDOR) contracted with the University of Nebraska–Lincoln faculty to do an assessment for the state. NDOR representatives were interested in using the study to get a better understanding of truck parking there. They were open to our suggestion of adding qualitative field research to the investigation.

The FHWA, in association with the Science Applications International Corporation (SAIC), developed an assessment model for states to determine if there was a deficiency of truck parking. The model assumed that the deficiency is determined by comparing the demand for parking to the supply of parking. Truck parking demand was assumed to be "for a highway segment based on total truck-hours of travel and the time and duration of stops" and the model quantifies the supply of truck parking spaces by looking at the number and location of public and private truck spaces. [22]

The research model required each state to follow a four-task outline to identify relevant trucking corridors, select analysis segments, and estimate parking demand; to inventory public and private parking space supply for each analysis segment; to identify deficiencies by comparing truck parking demand to parking supply; and to analyze the results.

A significant oversight in the SAIC model was that it looked only at the estimated number of trucks compared to the identified number of parking spaces, while ignoring the practice of how and where truck drivers actually parked their trucks. As everyone knows who has visited a truck stop or rest area, truck drivers do not always methodically park their trucks in designated parking stalls.

We used the mandated SAIC truck parking demand model and added complete observations of strategic Nebraska truck stops and rest areas to see if the way truck drivers parked their trucks indeed influenced the perception that the truck parking area was full. In accordance with SAIC's Tasks 1 and 2, we used Interstate America's Truck Stops Database in association with the travel guide The Trucker's Friend to identify truck stops and rest areas and their parking capacities. We employed two different research strategies to help assess truck parking demand and surveyed both truck stop operators and truck drivers. The assessments from the two surveys were quite different. Owners of truck stops on the western section of I-80 (the major interstate that runs east–west through the state) were more likely to respond that night-time parking was at capacity, in comparison to owners from the central and eastern section of the interstate. More than half of the truck drivers surveyed felt that there was not enough truck parking in all of Nebraska.

Results from Task 3 produced both diverging and converging observations as opposed to those found in Tasks 1 and 2. Working in accordance with the SAIC truck parking demand model, we inputted traffic, number of stalls, and speed data (among others) into the evaluation model. Contrary to what the truck stop operators observed, the truck parking demand model documented that the overall truck parking supply meets demand in Nebraska. This "overall" assessment is a bit misleading when the data become further disaggregated into truck parking demand for truck stops versus rest areas. The SAIC demand model showed a total shortfall for all Nebraska rest areas, while highlighting excess capacity at truck stops for the entire state. The parking demand model largely converged with the survey indicating that there is a shortage of truck parking at western I-80 rest areas. We looked to the direct observation field research of truck stops and rest areas to make sense out of the divergent observations between the supply study and demand study.

A team of two went to 10 truck parking areas to conduct the direct observation research. They observed six sites on I-80 (three rest areas and three truck stops) and two sites (one rest area and one truck stop) at Highway 2 and Highway 81. The research goal was to complement the truck stop operator and trucker surveys and the parking demand model to provide a more holistic understanding of the commercial vehicle parking demand in Nebraska. The surveys highlighted that evening truck parking was the most crowded, so the teams observed truck stops and rest areas between 8:00 p.m. and 7:00 a.m. The field researchers recorded two statistics: total parking use and overflow use. Total parking use accounts for the percentage of trucks parked at the observed site in relation to the number of available parking stalls. Overflow use describes the percentage of trucks parked at the entrance and exits (or other illegal locations) divided by the number of stalls at the site.

The I-80 direct observations provided the most noteworthy data, revealing that there was less parking available to trucks in the western section of the state than in the eastern section. In addition, all rest areas were operating at a higher capacity than truck stops. The levels of over-capacity achieved at some of the western I-80 rest areas proved very interesting. For example, as illustrated in Figure 2.4, the Brady Rest Area was operating consistently at overflow capacity from 11:00 p.m. to 7:00 a.m., with a peak overflow utilization of 140 percent at 4:00 a.m.

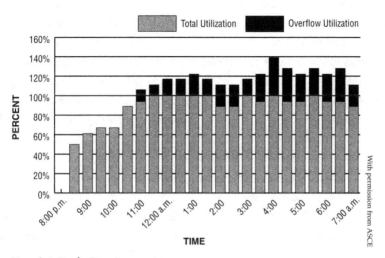

Figure 2.4 Brady Rest Area

The overflow parking at this rest area was somewhat evenly distributed at both the entrance and the exit, with slightly more trucks parked at the exit than the entrance.

The direct observations of the Nebraska truck stops and rest areas suggest that more truck parking may be needed in western Nebraska. Without directly observing the behavior of truck drivers, the researchers would have no knowledge of dangerous illegal parking at the entrances and exits of truck parking facilities. This important information would have been ignored if the Nebraska investigators strictly adhered to the SAIC research model. In addition to revealing the need to build new rest areas, the direct observations added interesting insights into the design of rest areas. The extreme overflow utilization statistics recorded at the Brady Rest Area, when the rest area was not at full capacity, highlights the need for better parking design—both so truck drivers can more easily park their vehicles and so more trucks can get in and park in the actual rest area rather than at the entrance or exit.

INTEGRATING TECHNOLOGY WITH FIELD RESEARCH TECHNOLOGIES

Tablet

Tablet computers (tablets) have become a standard day-to-day computing tool used by planners regardless of whether are conducting field research. Tablets are great for accessing information, recording data, and performing integrative analysis. Each of these applications has its own particular interface with each type of research strategy discussed in this chapter. (See Table 2.5.) Tablets allow the planner to access and send both stored information and information on the web and to make more informed tactical decisions when confronted with unanticipated events in the field. For example, if you are conducting site reconnaissance in an urban neighborhood and are finding very inconsistent land uses, you can use a tablet to access the city's web page and pull up the city's zoning map to determine if the observed land uses in the field conform to the city's zoned land use for the area.

There are several free and modest fee-based apps for the tablet that make the planner's clipboard obsolete for recording field data. There are a handful of field notebook apps that allow you to record and organize field notes, take images from the field and embed them in your field notes. In fact, some field notebook apps allow you to share your notes and images in real-time with your planning team while in the field. (You can also send screenshots from your tablet to have

Table 2.5 Tablet PC Field Research Applications

	Interface	Research Strategy	Application
Accessing Information	Access stored information	a. windshield survey b. site reconnaissance c. complete observations d. structured/ semistructured interviews	Pulling up stored information to help the planner in the field to make informed decisions
	Access internet information	a. windshield survey b. site reconnaissance c. complete observations d. structured/ semistructured interviews	Pulling up information off the web to help the planner in the field to make informed decisions
Recording Data	Experiential observations	a. windshield survey b. site reconnaissance c. complete observations d. unstructured observations	Quickly noting observed events, comments, research ideas for later analysis
	Qualitative observations	a. windshield survey b. site reconnaissance c. complete observations	Recording observed data into predeveloped field data files
	Interview observations	a. structured/ semistructured interviews	Recording observed data into predeveloped questionnaire spreadsheet file
Integrative Analysis	Recording/ integrating/ analyzing data	a. windshield survey b. site reconnaissance c. complete observations	Conducting GIS research while in the field; downloading data from a server; and analyzing field data with downloaded data

a digital record of your field entry.) Tablets are a good labor-saving device for recording quantitative observations and interview data. If you need to count items in the field (for example, the number of trucks parked in a rest area) you can directly input the data into a spreadsheet on the tablet. This eliminates the time-consuming process of entering data from the hardcopy field tally sheets into a digital spreadsheet. With larger tablet displays (larger than 10 inch displays), you can use still or video images imbedded in your field interview surveys. An indirect benefit to digitally collecting data in the field is that it helps avoid transcribing errors when inputting hardcopy information field notes to spreadsheets.

Planners have been integrating some GIS applications with their tablets with modest results. Here, planners have been mostly updating georeferenced data from the field to the cloud. The limitation of tablets' computing capacity, combined with small viewing screens and limited storage capacity, makes robust GIS analysis in the field very difficult. There are some kernel GIS software applications on the market that are small enough to run on a tablet, but they are very limited in how much detailed analysis the planner can execute in the field. Hopefully, bigger and more powerful tablets that can run a full-scale GIS software package will come on the market in the next few years providing planners with more options in uploading and downloading spatial data and analyzing it while still in the field.

The sharing of information between tablets and remote cloud-based servers raises some risks of compromise to uploaded files and more significant risks and management problems with issues of data privacy. Cloud computing is when storage providers provide third party data storage for paying customers and are commonly linked with field research apps. There is a remote risk that the cloud provider's physical server may crash. (It is always advisable to keep a second hard-drive copy of all field research data to protect you from the loss of data by a cloud provider.) A much more significant risk and management dilemma is a security breach in the cloud service where an unauthorized person gains access to all of the stored data in the cloud server. This presents a significant data management problem when the planner is generating Personal Identifiable Information (PII) data: data that can be used to isolate an individual's identity (e.g. birth date) or information that connects an individual to their health, education, financial, and employment data points. There are very clear Institutional Review Board (IRB) guidelines on what types of PII data are allowed to be synched with a cloud service and what measures (e.g. data encryption) are needed to be taken to insure the privacy of these data.

DISCUSSION QUESTIONS

1. The most significant benefit in unobtrusive investigations is that the planner is more able to minimize their presence in the community in hopes of capturing, as best as they can, the true essence of what is going on in the community. Can you see any added level of internal validity benefits for the planner by being able to provide "I was there" observational data?

2. The four identified field research techniques (windshield survey, site reconnaissance, complete observation, and physical trace analysis) are distinct from each other because they each take a particular approach to geographic scale and detail of observations. How would you go about connecting all four of the field research strategies into one

continuous flow of field observations starting from a windshield survey, then bringing it down to site reconnaissance, then focusing in on a specific area in the community, and ending up on a very close-up physical trace analysis? What do you think would be gained by connecting very small intimate community insights to a larger regional perspective?

3. Field research observations are most commonly applied when a planner needs to get up-to-date information about a particular place. Can you see the long-term value of going back to a past field research site over the course of a handful of years to provide longitudinal accounts of how the research site has changed over time? How would you record and catalog your field observations so that the next generation of planners in your office can access your longitudinal field research findings?

NOTES

i   Portions of this discussion appeared in: John Gaber, Sharon Gaber, Jeff Vincent, and Boellstorff Darcy. 2004. "An analysis of refugee resettlement patterns in the Great Plains," *Great Plains Research*, 14(2), pp. 165–184.

ii Portions of this discussion appeared in: Sharon Gaber, John Gaber, and Aemal Khattak. 2005. "Commercial truck parking analysis: Method to the madness or madness to the method?" *Journal of Urban Planning and Development*, 131(1), pp. 50–56.

REFERENCES

[1] Peattie, L. 1967. "The social anthropologists in planning," *Journal of American Institute of Planning*, 33(4), p. 267.

[2] Gans, H. 1982. *The Urban Villagers* (updated edition). New York: The Free Press, p. 417.

[3] Dewey, J. 1981. *The Latter Works, 1925–1953*, edited by A. Boydston. Carbondale, IL: Southern Illinois Press.

[4] Dandekar, H. (ed.). 2003. *The Planner's Use of Information*. Chicago, IL: Planners Press, p. 31.

[5] Dandekar, *Planner's Use*, p. 30.

[6] Dandekar, *Planner's Use*, pp. 30–32.

[7] Whyte, W. 1988. *City, Rediscovering the Center*. New York: Anchor Books, p. 4.

[8] Whyte, *City*, pp. 58–59.

[9] Whyte, *City*, p. 1.

[10] Denzin, N. 1989. *The Research Act* (3rd ed.). Englewood Cliffs, NJ: Prentice Hall, p. 69.

[11] Levy, J. 2003. *Contemporary Urban Planning* (6th ed.). Upper Saddle River, NJ: Prentice Hall, p. 198.

[12] Webb, E., Campbell, D., Schwartz, R., and Sechrest, L. 1966. *Unobtrusive Measures: Nonreactive Research in the Social Sciences*. Chicago, IL: Rand McNally & Co.

[13] Corburn, J. 2005. *Street Science: Community Knowledge and Environmental Health Justice*. Cambridge, MA: MIT Press.

[14] Bailie, R., and Stevens, E.L. 2012. "The impact of housing improvement and socio-environmental factors on common childhood illness: a cohort study in Indigenous Australian communities," *Journal of Epidemiology and Community Health*, 66(9), pp. 821–831, p. 824.

[15] Bailie and Stevens, "Impact", p. 830.

[16] Creswell, J. 1994. *Research Design*. Thousand Oaks, CA: Sage Publications; Miles, M., and Huberman, M. 1984. *Qualitative Data Analysis: A Sourcebook of New Methods*, Beverly Hills, CA: Sage; and Schatzman, L., and Anselm S. 1973. *Field Research*. Englewood Cliffs, NJ: Prentice Hall.

[17] Shatzman, L., and Strauss. A. 1973. *Field Research: Strategies for Natural Science*. Englewood Cliffs, NJ: Prentice Hall.

[18] Zukin, S. 1989. *Loft Living*. New Brunswick, NJ: Rutgers University Press.

[19] Portes, A. 1987. "The social origins of the Cuban enclave economy in Miami," in *Sociological Perspectives*, 30(October), pp. 340–372.

[20] Portes, A., and Manning, R. 1986. "The immigrant enclave: Theory and empirical examples," in *Competitive Ethnic Relations*, edited by B. S. Olzak, and J. Nagel. New York: Academic Press, p. 63.

[21] Light, I., and Bonacich, E. 1988. *Immigrant Entrepreneurs*. Berkeley, CA: University of California Press.

[22] Federal Highway Administration. 2002. *Study of Adequacy of Commercial Truck Parking Facilities* (technical report).

3

PHOTOGRAPHIC RESEARCH

WHAT IS PHOTOGRAPHIC RESEARCH?

Research photographs capture images that provide empirical information to other data sets or to an established theory. Photographs used as part of research differ markedly from photographs used as illustration. The empirical value of photographic research requires the images to be obtained through a methodological process indexed to recognizable objects and spatial variables. When placed in the context of systematic recording within a field research methodology, photographs become "independent specimens of data." [1] On the other hand, photographs used as illustrations provide only visual confirmation of something that exists (or existed or happened), with no connection to other data sets or established theory. Illustrative images depict a condition or place, with the goals of helping others visualize different scenarios, communicating ideas, and even persuading the public to take action. [2]

All photographic research requires you to show a visually understandable image of the research subject to allow careful contemplation and analysis, avoiding images that have artistic presentations, unusual vistas (points of view), or distorted juxtapositions of visual variables that overemphasize a particular perspective. Second, visual variables depicted in an empirical photograph must be informed by theory. Theory in photographic research explains why visual variables are important. Finally, identifiable visual variables need to be spatially indexed to other visual variables in the image. [3] Non-theoretically informed visual variables either show little or no relationship to other variables or have little theoretical explanation about the contextual relevancy among the other visual variables. If you do it correctly, you will be like a radiologist taking and reading an x-ray; you take images of a research subject to learn more about what is going on in the community.

WHY DO PLANNERS NEED PHOTOGRAPHIC RESEARCH?

The planner uses research-framed photographic images like a physicist uses mathematical calculations—to provide the visual evidence of systematic knowledge in relation to a particular planning problem. [4] Dramatic examples are the images Jacob Riis took of the horrible slum conditions on New York's Lower East Side in his book, *How the Other Half Lives*, published in 1890. [5] Riis was able to visually record the deplorable immigrant tenement housing conditions and this eventually led to the much-needed social reforms of the 1900s.

Photographic investigations also allow you to capture complex situations with the click of a shutter. Unlike most quantitative-based research approaches, where you need to input all of your numbers into a spreadsheet or GIS, photographic research allows you to go directly to the research site, see obviously significant events, places, or people, and capture the situation in an image. Photographic research lets you know precisely what you have captured (especially with a digital camera), while the quantitative research planner has to return to the office, organize, and analyze the data before coming up with (basically) the same observation. This approach does not mean you don't have to carefully analyze your images. As we will see later in this chapter, you must carefully decode empirical images for a more detailed understanding and application of what was captured in them.

There are two other compelling reasons why you may choose photographic investigations. First, you have the option to enter into the physical context of the research topic. Here, you are an "eyewitness" to an event, and your images are proof that you were actually there. This allows you to speak from personal experience about the images: "When I took this photograph …" Second, investigative images can be extremely powerful in influencing public opinion. In fact, Riis used his images of the Lower East Side specifically to promote social reform in New York City.

WHEN DO PLANNERS USE PHOTOGRAPHIC RESEARCH?

An infinite number of research situations will lead you to do photographic investigations. Collier and Collier help planners conceptualize this line of exploration by identifying three broad genres of visually based investigations that cover the most common photographic research situations: Mapping and survey, cultural inventories and documentation of social process, and counting and measuring. (See Table 3.1.)

Table 3.1 Three Genres of Photographic Research Commonly Used by Planners

	Genre	Definition	Vista	Planning Application
1. Mapping and Surveying	Mapping	Large-scale images of cultural, economic, social, and political geography	Aerial	Aerial images to analyze uses (Hayden, 2000[a])
	Survey	Eye-level images of a community or landscape	Images of structures, objects, people in relation to their immediate environment	Images of abandoned buildings in an economically depressed section of town (Reader, 1998[b], 2000[c])
2. Cultural Inventories and Social Process	Cultural Inventories	Images of how people use their everyday spaces	Up-close images of people in their immediate space	Images of how older women use a particular space (Chua, 1991[d])
	Social Process	Images of social events	Eye-level images of people in their immediate and contextual space	Immigrant laborers working in a seat shop (Riis, 1890)
3. Counting and Measuring	Counting and Measuring	An image that records the history, size, or number of events	Can range from panoramic aerial to extremely close-up images	Large-scale images of how people use urban spaces to small-scale images of how people walk up steps (Whyte, 1988[e])

[a] Hayden, D. 2000. "Flying over Guilford," Planning, 66(9), September, 10–15.
[b] Reardon, K. 1998. "Enhancing the capacity of community-based organizations in East St. Louis," Journal of Planning Education and Research, 17:4, 323–333.
[c] Reardon, K. 2000. "Down on the River," Planning, 66(9), September, 20–23.
[d] Chua, B.H. 1991. "Modernism and Vernacular: Transformation of Public Spaces and Social Life in Singapore," Journal of Architecture and Planning Research, 8:3, 203–222.
[e] Whyte, W. 1988. City, Rediscovering the Center, New York: NY, Doubleday Books.

Mapping and survey photographic investigations are the most common. This genre of research looks at visual variables that are informed by theory at a specific location, such as photographing different hurricane measures of development (theory) along the western coast of Florida (location). In mapping, the planner takes large-scale or aerial images of the landscape. One example is an aerial image of residential development in relation to local factories.

Photographic survey research takes an eye-level view—"This is what I see"—of a particular community or location. An image of empty storefronts in the central business district is one example.

Planners have used the camera as a counting and measuring tool much more often in the last five years with the growing affordability of drones. Here, planners use images for statistical analysis, either to count the number of times an event occurs (for example, number of cars in a parking lot) or to measure the magnitude or changing magnitude of an activity (suburban residential development moving into neighboring farmland).

Planners use photographic research to document cultural inventories and social processes infrequently, mainly because of the amount of time it takes to develop a relationship with the research subjects necessary to be able to capture this type of image. Both of these investigations strive to obtain images that show an "insider's view" of a place or activity. Cultural inventories are images of people's intimate spaces (for example, a bedroom, homeless encampment, truck driver cab). Images of social process depict the interaction of people (or animals) with each other (for example, people simultaneously entering and exiting a subway car).

DOING PHOTOGRAPHIC RESEARCH

Visually based research is the methodological process that purposefully freezes a split-second of time to capture a data slice in the form of an image. Getting the "right" image requires you to know not only what you are looking at, but also what framed image you're looking for. You should leave nothing to chance. After you get the images, you must carefully decode them to better understand and communicate how the images contribute to the overall research project.

Setting Up

Photographic research is very similar to field research; you go out to gather observations. In this case, however, your primary objective is to capture images from the field and support them with descriptive text explaining why the images are significant. In field research, you primarily search for detailed experiential data from the field, adding a few images to support your observations and explaining how an image captures the essence of the field research. But like the field researcher, the photographic researcher needs to do a significant amount of work to set up the photographic investigation beforehand.

Assuming you have a clear sense of the research question, you need to complete three tasks before going out to get your images: (1) identify the visual variables, (2) previsualize (as explained below) the type of images needed, and (3) develop a shooting guide. Before taking the images, you need to know the variables you are searching for. Variables in photographic research are very different from other types of research variables because they must be seen through a camera—or at least evidence of the variable must be seen through a camera. Visual variables are obvious to you because you can see them, but it takes "creative seeing" to capture evidence of variables not easily seen. An image of a tall mountain where the altitude of the mountain is highlighted by evidence of the tree line in relation to the peak is an example of visual evidence.

To begin, develop a rough image in your mind's eye of what the photo should look like through the process of previsualization. First, visualize the research site within a larger context. Images of the research site, georeferenced to recognizable local or regional landmarks (for example, distant skyline, backdrop of mountains, major intersection), put the place of interest in the context of a larger community, region, or landscape. Next, visualize the site as a tableau. This conceptualization requires you to see the site as a series of immediate landmarks that identify the research site as a place. Examples are a corner grocery store, a river's edge, a street sign, or neighborhood park. Next, visualize the primary subjects in each image. What are the main visual variables in each image? How are these variables organized? How do the various variables work?

Last, decide whose point of view you want the image to reflect. These are the vistas you choose. Everything in life looks a little bit different depending on how someone sees the environment. You need to think about visualizing the research site from both an "insider's" vista as well as an "outsider's" view, looking in. Capturing images with an "insider's" perspective is another way to inject the community's perspective in your research and plan-making activities.

A shooting guide will help you better organize your time in the field. [6] This guide, like an interview guide in focus group research, identifies all the images you need to take, and identifies the more important ones. The guide should identify location, primary visual variables, variable composition, and the different vistas per image. The shooting guide provides only overall direction for the various shots, though, and you should feel free to improvise if you discover new and more insightful images during the process.

Getting the Data

Executing photographic research is a very mechanical process: you go to the research site and start taking images. Below the surface, though, these activities are more complicated. The scale of images you are interested in determines how you go about taking your shots. Large-scale images (usually mapping, counting, and measuring types of images) can range from shots of a couple of buildings to an entire streetscape, skyline, or aerial photographs of whole regions. Given the macroperspective of these types of images, you won't have to worry much about how you will interact with the community—you'll spend more time thinking about how to capture the shot.

As the scale of the image comes down to more of a human scale, like storefronts, a handful of people standing on a street corner, or people waiting to catch their morning bus to work, how you plan to enter the research site and negotiate permission to take images gets much more complicated. When you shoot images at eye level, the subject's veil of anonymity is dropped. Here, the images are intimate and personal. Before you proceed, you must obtain permission to take photographs of both people and objects. If the images are very close up, as they are in cultural inventories or social process images, you'll need to invest a good amount of ethnographic field research time with your subjects to earn their trust and to gain a better understanding of what visual variables need to be captured in the images.

The composition of the image adds complexity: How should you arrange the visual variables in the viewfinder so what you see in the field appears in the image? To answer this, I will briefly discuss image composition, camera perspective, and camera angles.

Image composition is the visual organization of important variables so that another person seeing the photograph can see and understand what you saw in the field. Since most planners are not formally trained in image composition or visual literacy, more often than not you will find yourself taking a photograph of a single variable and centering it in the middle of the image. When you want to capture more than one variable to improve the readability of your images,

Figure 3.1 "Rule of Thirds"

employ the "Rule of Thirds": Divide an image into thirds with two equally spaced horizontal and vertical lines (see Figure 3.1). The best place to position important variables is at one of the four points where the lines intersect. The points of intersection are called "power points" and are where the eye naturally falls on the image.

The distance between the photographer and the main variables defines the camera perspective, known as the "shot" in photographic terminology. There are four types of common shots (Table 3.2). Most importantly, different shots create different effects upon the subject matter. The farther away you are from the main variables, the more of the environment and context is shown in the image, providing the viewer a sense of action and/or place. The closer you get to the main variables, the more intimate the image becomes to the viewer, making the image more dramatic and personal.

The camera angle (what I call vista) reflects the relationship of the photographer to the research subject. When the camera is higher and farther away from the research variables (for example, in aerial photographs), the vista provides a

Table 3.2 Common Camera Perspective Shots

Type of Shot	Distance	Effect	Planning Application
Long Shot	Photographer far from variable(s). Variables fill only a small part of the image.	Variable(s) in context for action or environment	Aerial images of land-use patterns
Medium Shot	Photographer at a common distance to variable(s). Variable(s) fill up the entire image.	Clear sense of details in variable(s) in relation to immediate context	Images of streetscapes, neighborhoods, public parks
Close-up Shot	Photographer close to variable(s). Variable(s) fill up the entire image.	Tremendous detail in variable(s)	A person, factory, storefront, park bench
Extreme Close-up Shot	Photographer moves past the personal space of variable(s). Only part of the variable fills the image.	Intense emotion and drama	Part of a face, back of a vehicle, front door to a church, an artifact

birds-eye view of the subject, which tends to be removed and "all-knowing." Camera shots taken at an eye-level angle in medium- to close-range provide a more personal understanding of the variables. Images taken from inside the community according to a "local view" provide visually based data as seen through the eyes of local residents. It is generally a good rule of thumb to secure as many angles and vistas of the same variables as possible to get the many different views of the same subject—local neighborhood residents see growing residential traffic very differently from how a commuter sees the same situation.

As I explain in the next section, from a data-management perspective, it is imperative that you keep a simple tally of how many images you take and their locations every time you go out into the field. These shooting field notes require only a piece of paper and pen and can be completed while you are in the field or shortly after leaving.

Organizing the Data

The ease of shooting empirical images is the calm before the storm leading up to organizing the same images for analysis. Photographic research requires you to take a tremendous number of images. More significantly, a higher number of images provides more choices for picking the best empirical image that, in fact, "says a thousand words." This is better than sifting through a few so-so images to get an image that says a handful of words, at best. But the motivation to capture the right image can also result in a potential management nightmare of organizing dozens, hundreds, and even thousands of images for analysis.

To avoid such confusion, use your shooting guide to organize your images before you take them. While shooting the images, keep track of how many images you took, where you took them, and when. The combination of the shooting guide and the shooting field notes provides the organizational structure to organize the images. Each photographic expedition needs to be isolated from other expeditions and categorized by date, place, and if necessary, photographer. Within each expedition, all the images must be organized in sequential order per shot. One of the subtle joys of working with a digital camera is that all of the images captured with this tool are encoded with the date and time. This feature dramatically makes sequencing the images much easier.

Analyzing the Data

Analyzing empirical photographic images can be done quickly when you only have a few images; are operating on a tight time frame; or need only to provide the most basic observations. On the other hand, if you have volumes of images and need to provide a very detailed analysis, you'll require more time for review. Use the research question that prompted the photographic research in the first place to go over all the images in chronological order, picking out shots that directly speak to the question and other data sets in the overall research project. If you are interested only in a simple analysis of the images, you can quickly pick a short list of the best images and do a simple write-up of how the images contribute to the research project. This analysis simply decodes visual variables into statistical or written observations and should include a direct identification of the variables and why they are significant (for example, buildings, sidewalks, streets); a brief highlight of some of the more prominent components of these variables (for example, building types, width of the sidewalk, the number of lanes on the street); and if possible, a short discussion of some of the obvious functions they serve (for example, zoning, public open space, traffic). [7] After this quick analysis, you can choose the most prominent images for the final report or public presentation.

For a more detailed analysis of images, compare and contrast them, looking at the chronological evolution of images over time. Look for similarities and dissimilarities in the ways the variables are presented in the images. For example, do some areas of a community have higher building density, more traffic congestion, or larger numbers of people walking on the sidewalk in comparison to other places in the research site that are just a few blocks away from the original shoot?

When you analyze the chronological evolution of images, you will look at a series of photographs to see if any of the visual variables have changed over time. If you're lucky, and you know that a series of changes are about to take place at a specific location, you can capture "before and after" images of the research site to document the change. For example, Herbert Gans documented Boston's West End before and after the tight-knit Italian community was virtually wiped off the map by urban renewal to make way for the upscale Charles River Place project. [8] More often than not, though, you won't be so lucky. You will have to look more closely at your images to document and analyze more subtle variable changes at the research site.

Collecting an image library of landscapes, cities, communities, and neighborhoods establishes a visual base of how places look and function in the past and the present. Converting old photographs into digital images and using digital cameras for current and future photographic investigations makes storing the images extremely cost-effective (the images can be stored on existing computers or servers) and takes up no additional office space. Planning research and plan-making possibilities would be limitless if cities, universities, and national and local planning organizations each established image libraries that could be accessed via the Internet.

"Microanalysis," as termed by Collier and Collier, [9] describes the finest-grain, most time-consuming analysis. This is a very detailed inspection of the images as you look for the subtlest insights. Here, you contemplate the images loosely from a Roland Barthes approach and look at the images for both their denotations (what the images show) and connotations (what the images imply). [10] This level of analysis becomes contemplative and moves to the subject of conversation (what the image means) as opposed to being the subject of evidence for a research project, where the image is a specimen of data that addresses questions. Planners seldom conduct this level of analysis for public meetings, where time is limited. Microanalysis is usually initiated by universities.

QUESTIONS OF INTERNAL AND EXTERNAL VALIDITY AND ISSUES OF RELIABILITY IN PHOTOGRAPHIC RESEARCH

As a data-gathering tool, the camera is very reliable and fairly free of intrinsic biases because of its mechanical process of capturing images. But when the photographer is behind the viewfinder, questions of internal and external validity and reliability become more problematic. Internal validity is by far the most difficult test for photographic investigations to pass. Since visually based research is premised on seeing, how it addresses questions of internal and external validity and reliability is very different from how more verbally based qualitative research (for example, focus groups) addresses the same questions.

Questions of Internal Validity

The basic question of internal validity in photographic research is: Did the planner correctly represent and interpret the visual variables in the photograph? The lack of internal validity in visually based research rests on three junctures: (1) the mechanical capturing of images; (2) the proper (or improper and exploitative) context of capturing images; and (3) the correct composition and analysis of images. (See Table 3.3.) By questioning photographs, internal validity moves the methodological reference of image-based research from a positivistic frame of analysis—"pictures cannot lie"—to a dialogical assessment, making the empirical value of images rest on the planner's ability to both capture and communicate what is going on in the photographs. [11]

You will need to address two mechanical shortcomings in the camera that threaten internal validity. The "two-dimensional/three-dimensional divide" [12] describes the camera's optical system, which translates three-dimensional reality into a two-dimensional image. As this happens, the spatial relationship of visual variables is altered, jeopardizing the indexality of the image. How visual variables look three-dimensionally in relation to each other in real life is different than how they are depicted two-dimensionally in an image. To combat this optical threat to validity, take several images from multiple vistas to show, to the best of your ability, the three-dimensional characteristics of the research site. Also, educate your audience and explain that you do not expect your images to duplicate reality as they personally experience it. There is a big difference in how we "see" an image versus how we "see" in real life. [13] Photographs, like spreadsheets, represent reality only through resemblance, and in the case of photographs, in two dimensions and not three.

Table 3.3 Common Questions of Internal Validity in Photographic Research

	Type of Question	Problem	Example	Solution
1. Mechanical	A. 2D/3D Divide	Inaccurate depiction of three-dimensional variables	Image of main street storefronts as a flat wall	Take several images from various vistas to show the three-dimensional aspect of visual variables
	B. Split-Second in Time	Unrepresentative image of the everyday depiction of variables	Image of low traffic volume on a street that usually has high traffic	Takes several images at various times and on different days
2. Context/ Exploitation	A. Us versus Them	Unfair depiction of people or places	Images of homeless people standing in line for food	a) Get permission to shoot image. b) Spend time in the field to earn the image.
3. Composition and Interpretation	A. Wrong Analysis/Accurate Image	Poor understanding of research variables. Planner did not know what she was seeing.	Images of poor residents as despondent and dangerous	Get a better understanding of the research variables before shooting
	B. Wrong Analysis/ Inaccurate Image	a) Improper image composition b) Improper camera perspective; and/or c) Improper vista	Image of street vendors depicted as an impediment to pedestrian traffic	a) Take images from various vistas and perspectives. b) Get a better understanding of the research variables.
	C. Wrong Analysis/ Improper Image Editing of Variables	Improper manipulation of image (cropping, spatial/ sizing manipulation, coloring, introduction of new variables)	Adding proposed buildings, streetscape, pedestrians to an image	a) "If it ain't real, it ain't empirical". b) Use image editing sparingly. c) If image editing is used, the

Shooting a photograph is a "hundredth-of-a-second slice of reality" that freezes "a specific moment in time and space." [14] This presents a very significant problem. Is a photograph worth contemplation and is it representative of reality? Or is it only a fleeting moment in time, never to happen again? You can fairly easily address this question of internal validity by taking several pictures of the research site, cross-referencing visually based data to other data sets for validation, and taking video images of the research site to show the observed variables and how they operate on a typical day.

Photographic research has the ability to be exploitative, presenting another substantive challenge to internal validity. Photographic images, no matter how accurately they portray the subject matter, can be extremely exploitative by framing the subject in the wrong context. Photographic investigations tend to have a dualistic nature. The camera separates the planner from community by putting her in the role of the viewer/researcher and the community into the role of the viewed/subject. The camera becomes a research tool "that allows 'us' to understand more about 'them.'" [15] You can easily avoid the pitfalls of photographic investigations by getting permission from people or places before you shoot your image. Ask the subjects if it is O.K. to take their images and explain to them why you are taking them. You need to conduct yourself in an ethical way so your future audience can trust that you took the time to talk with the subjects before you took the photos. If you cannot get permission, either don't take the shot or take an image that accurately frames the subject (for example, being homeless) but preserves the anonymity of the individual. Often, you will get permission to take photos after you have established a rapport with your subjects. You can earn a subject's trust and confidence that the images will not be used for personal gain or to the detriment of either the person or the place.

Errors in image composition and interpretation can negatively affect internal validity. In this case you might incorrectly interpret an accurate image, incorrectly interpret an inaccurate image, or incorrectly interpret an improperly edited image. What all three of these mistakes have in common is that you lacked the necessary knowledge about the research variables before shooting the image. As a result, you did not have a clear concept of what the variables meant when they were correctly or incorrectly portrayed in the image. This represents the classic mistake of shooting images first and asking research-related questions later. All good photographic investigations should be grounded with the planner doing her homework about the visual variables, and then asking questions before, during, and after all the images have been shot in the field. Visual-based research is an ongoing investigation, not a conclusion.

Improper image editing is a rising concern because it affects the empirical application of photographic research. Additionally, the simplicity and prevalence of photo manipulation software makes this a very real risk. The planning profession is currently wrestling to determine at what point the manipulation of an image crosses the line to what it is equivalent to "cooking the numbers," or altering the empirical value of the photographic to better fit the research objective. Based on the information presented in this chapter, you can more clearly delineate this ethical line by asking three questions about the image. If you can answer "yes" to any of the three questions, the image editing has crossed over the line to being an invalid manipulation of data: (1) Does the manipulation of the image change the everyday depiction of the visual variables? Is the sky bluer, or are people, buildings, cars, trees added or removed from the image? (2) Does the manipulation of the image change what the visual variables communicate to theory or other data sets? Are some variables shaded or lightened to emphasize or deemphasize their significance in the image? (3) Does the manipulation of the image change the spatial indexality of the visual variables onto itself or to other variables? Are some variables increased in size while other variables are shrunk, or are some variables completely eliminated through overly aggressive cropping of the image?

It is easier to diagnostically determine what is considered acceptable and unacceptable image editing procedure by clearly comparing the three basic characteristics of an empirical image (easily identifiable image, theory-informed framework directing the type of images shot, and spatially indexed visual variables) to how the image was manipulated. For example, if an image of a urban corridor filled with buildings on a busy street with heavy pedestrian traffic is manipulated so that all of the cars and people are removed from the image, it is a violation of the spatially indexed characteristic of empirical images because the spatial relationship of the buildings to the cars and the pedestrian traffic has been changed. The new view of the corridor no longer resembles how people commonly understand and experience the space. This commonly used practice by urban designers and architects moves the urban corridor image from that of empirical data (buildings, cars, and pedestrians) to that of an illustration of the buildings alone.

Questions of External Validity

Questions of external validity focus on the planner's ability to connect an image to the larger theoretical and empirical ramifications in the research project: how does this image directly advance our understanding about a specific research question or data set?

Threats to external validity in photographic research can occur in one of two ways. First, you may not provide an adequate explanation about how the image relates to the research project. Adequately explaining the importance of an image is basic to photojournalism.

Of the simpler ingredients of subject matter in the photojournalistic complex, the who, the where, and the when are questions answered by the photograph only in part, if at all. Often the photograph is not fully clear with respect to the what and raises doubt or conjecture as to the why or how. In supplying or completing these answers the writer proves the need of his medium. He identifies people, locales, objects and establishes the relationships among them. He fixes the time of what is shown in the photograph. He confirms or corrects the reader's analysis of emotion and explains other obscurities. He supplies evidence of the other senses: sound, smell, taste, feel. [16]

The second threat to external validity happens when the planner inappropriately applies the visually based findings from one research site to another one. Empirical photographic observations made from one case study are not transitive to other case studies. However, the planner can use images from one research site as an example or illustration of what is being done at a different research site. But even then, using images from one location to better understand a different location is never a close fit. The presentations of these images usually "oversimplify and misrepresent" what is actually going on. [17]

Reliability

The camera is an extremely reliable machine. Assuming fixed camera settings (shutter speed, film, focal length), no matter who presses the shutter the camera will always take the same image. So the question of reliability in photographic research focuses on the planner taking the pictures and how images taken from uncommon vistas or points of view were obtained. "How did you get that shot?"

To address these concerns, you much provide a detailed prologue to your presentation to discuss how you got access to that particular vista to take the shot. (See Case Study #1 that follows to read my explanation for the photo "the shell game" on 14th Street.) Questions of reliability are most prevalent in photographic investigations where the planner needs to work closely with people or special environments, such as cultural inventories or social process investigations, or where unusual expenditures or equipment are needed to take the image, such as in photographic expeditions for mapping, counting, or measuring.

CASE STUDY #1: THE 14TH STREET VENDORS MARKETPLACE[I]

Planners are often confronted with a problem that has little or no literature to directly explain what is going on in the specific situation. In these original research opportunities, the planner goes to the research site armed with a handful of research tools and the closest related theory to figure out what is happening. In my investigation of street vendors peddling on 14th Street in Manhattan in the early 1990s, the only literature I could find was city ordinances and a handful of books on pushcart vendors during the Industrial Revolution. So, armed with the city's multiple street vendor ordinances dating back to 1916 and various theories on the informal economy, I set out to 14th Street to learn more.

I combined nine months of ethnographic field research of 14th Street with a photographic investigation. The research strategy was to start with the ethnographic investigation to gain acceptance by local shop owners and street vendors and, then, integrate photographic expeditions while I was in the field. The research focused on a two-block section of 14th Street because it had the highest concentration of street vendors. I took a combination of 219 black-and-white photographs and 83 color slides, totaling 302 images of the vendors.

The theory that guided the visual and ethnographic investigations was the research literature on the informal economy that distinguished informal economic activity from illicit economic activity. The informal economy is made up of all of those economic activities that are legal, but which are determined to be illegal by the government because they violate local laws or ordinances. It is illegal to peddle on 14th Street between Monday and Saturday, and the local street vendors (some of whom are licensed vendors otherwise) sell their legal merchandise illegally on those days. [18] This is in contrast to illicit activities that are outright illegal, such as selling stolen property. Our research focused on learning how and why informal street vending was taking place on 14th Street.

The type of photographic investigative approach I took was a combination of survey research—where I took eye-level images with long and medium shots of street vendors in relation to the overall sidewalk and storefronts (Figure 3.2), to themselves (Figure 3.3), and to each other (Figure 3.4)—and social process, where I took close-up, eye-level images of the vendors with their merchandise to get a better understanding about their trade (Figure 3.5).

Photographic investigations can have a powerful synergistic relationship with ethnographic research. My ethnographic investigation opened doors on 14th Street

Figure 3.2 Long Shot of 14th Street Vendors Marketplace

Figure 3.3 Eye-level Shot of 14th Street Vendor

Figure 3.4 Eye-level Shot of 14th Street Vendors Marketplace

that I would never had been accessed if I were shooting only images and had not engaged with the people on the street. For example, Figure 3.6 is an "inside" view of the shell game that local street hustlers played on 14th Street to trick people (mostly unsuspecting tourists) out of their money by getting them to bet which shell the pea was under. These games were always short-lived (no more than 10 to 15 minutes) because the police quickly came in, shut down the game, and vainly tried to catch the local hustlers. I got this shot as a result of our extensive ethnographic research, which allowed me to build a level of trust with the locals on the street.

Photographic investigations also can open doors for ethnographic research. After six months in the field, a Vietnamese vendor and his wife were still not interested in talking to me. One day I was taking photographs of vendors and they asked me to take their picture. After the picture was developed,

Figure 3.5 Close-up of 14th Street Immigrant Women Peddling

I gave them a copy. I had made a new relationship and a new vendor contact on 14th Street.

To decode street vendor images, I broke down the data to visual variables with clear functions. (See Table 3.4.) The basic variables in the images (Figures 3.3–3.6) are street vendors, storefronts, and pedestrians. These vendors can be organized

Figure 3.6 Close-up of 14th Street "Shell Game"

into types of peddlers: those who sell general merchandise; vendors who sell nonfood items from mobile carts or from carried bags; mobile food vendors, who sell food items from wheeled carts; and stoopline vendors who sell general merchandise from a rented space in the front vestibule of a store.

Table 3.4 Variable Decoding of 14th Street Vendors Market Images

Visual Variables	Variable Characteristics	Variable Functions
Street Vendors	Type of vendors: a) General merchanded mobile vendor; b) Mobile food vendor; c) Stoopline vendor	a) Source of income; b) Sale of affordable goods; c) Open-air bazaar shopping atmosphere
Pedestrian	Type of pedestrians: a) Shoppers and b) walkers	Contribute to open-air bazaar atmosphere
Storefronts	Type of stores: a) stores that welcome stoopline vendors b) Stores that do not take on stoopline vendors	a) Social and b) economic relationship with street vendors

The pedestrian variable is broken down into shoppers who are shopping at a specific store, people who are shopping at all the stores and vendors on 14th Street, and walkers who are on 14th Street on their way to a different destination. The storefront variable is made up of stores that allow vendors to rent stoopline space. Collectively, the functions of the three visual variables captured on 14th Street make up the "14th Street Vendors Market," where recent immigrants from different countries come to earn a living peddling or to shop for affordable goods. The general merchandise sold by the vendors is usually dated or suffers minor blemishes, making the market a type of clearinghouse for nationally recognized name-brand goods. The density of vendors coming together help to create a special open-air bazaar that attracts tourists and shoppers to the area.

CASE STUDY #2: RURAL HOUSING IN HALE COUNTY, ALABAMA

Hale County in Alabama's "Blackbelt" region has a dramatic shortage of livable housing. Mainly poor, African-American residents live in this rural county, which is still recovering from the abandoned plantation economy over a century ago. Currently, the county's residential units are collectively at five times the national average for substandard plumbing. Housing close to towns gets some attention from the state and from the Auburn University Rural Studio, which builds new homes and structures for disadvantaged residents. The houses on the outskirts of town and in the more remote regions in the county—virtually off the county, state, and nation's radar—need rehabilitation assistance. Photographic research would help people from outside the county to see and better understand living conditions there.

Hale County Housing Resource Center (HERO) is working to improve its rural housing conditions. HERO's director had a rough estimate of the number of houses in the county that needed work, but was not exactly sure of the locations and conditions of these houses. She contacted me to help her determine the exact location of some of the more remote houses in need of repair, renovation, or replacement, and to get an image of each house so she could easily identify it and have the visual data for further analysis.

New technology came to my assistance in this project. A new development in digital photography particularly applicable to planning is integration with GIS. Some digital cameras with respectable megapixel sizes (around 3.2) come with an extra expansion slot that integrates coordinates from a GPS (Global Positioning System) receiver. The camera "watermarks" each image with latitude, longitude, and elevation. The images can then be formatted with a GPS-photo link software that allows easy hot linking of images to ESRI ArcView software through the

ArcView extension. Clicking on the feature point in an ArcView map will display the georeferenced image.

The HERO director told me of three specific areas in the county that had the most impoverished living conditions; little was known about the existing housing stock. Going out to the community with the HERO director equipped with a GPS digital camera and a tablet PC, I visited each section of the county, using the camera as a counting device to enumerate each house in the three research areas and as a survey device to record the visual evidence of housing needs per house. The tablet PC was used to record additional observations for each photographed house, download images from the digital camera, and to make field notes to keep track of all the shots taken.

It took us one long day in July in the field to record all the houses in the three study areas. (See Figure 3.7.) I documented and mapped a total of 37 houses.

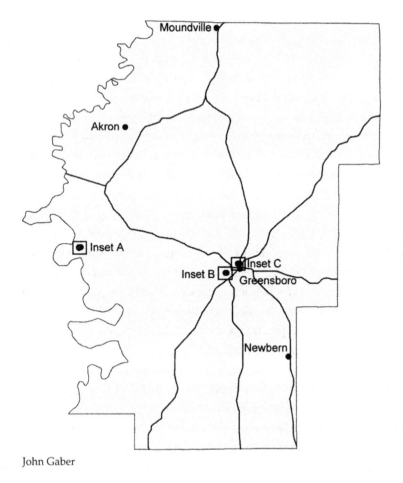

John Gaber

Figure 3.7 Three Study Areas in Hale County

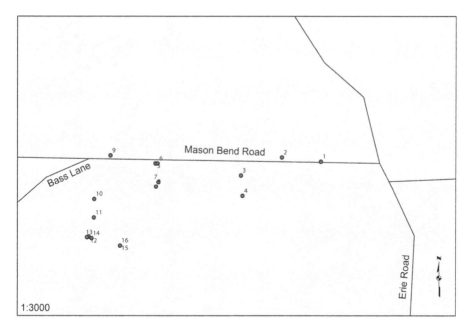

Figure 3.8 Insert A: Mason's Bend Cul-de-sacs

John Gaber

Figure 3.9 An Older Mobile Home

Figure 3.10 Permanent Housing

Figure 3.11 Evolving House

Anticipating that the houses needed more than one image to account for the multiple structural or site problems, I brought along an additional digital camera with a higher image quality for more detailed shots. The images of the houses allowed us to reflect on the visual characteristics of each house and identify its immediate structural characteristics. The georeferenced images were then integrated into a GIS analysis of Hale County.

HERO was particularly interested in housing conditions in the remote Mason's Bend area (Figure 3.8). A total of 16 residences were documented on or just off Mason's Bend Road. Housing in the area was either spread out or closely clustered into informal cul-de-sac settlements. Most of the structures in the area were mobile homes, with some fixed-site units and one "evolving" home. Here, each image is accompanied by a short description of the structural integrity of the home and the area immediately surrounding it.

INTEGRATING TECHNOLOGY WITH PHOTOGRAPHIC RESEARCH

Digital Photography

Digital photography has replaced film photography in applied planning applications. Two of the more important technical factors that you need to figure out before you begin your photographic investigation are digital image quality and type of digital camera you will use in the field. The digital camera operates almost identically to the traditional film camera with its lens, aperture, shutter, recording medium, and viewfinder, but the "medium" recording the captured image is in an electronic format rather than on film. Digital image quality is determined by the quality and intensity of pixels (short for "PICture Element," which stands for a single, square dot in an image). Assuming a good pixel resolution, the quality of a digital image is roughly measured by the number of megapixels (one million pixels per dot) with which the camera is able to record an image. The higher the megapixels, the more visual image information is recorded, resulting in a higher quality image. The current baseline for acceptable image resolution is at 8 megapixels; medium image resolution is at 16 to 24 megapixels; and high image resolution is at 45 megapixels or higher.

While you are thinking about megapixels and the quality of the image, you also need to keep in mind the memory size and storage method for each photo. Digital cameras store images on a memory card. As the number of megapixels goes up, so does the amount of memory needed to store the image. (See Table 3.5.) You need to seek a balance between the number of megapixels needed to capture

Table 3.5 Approximate Number of Recordable Images Per Memory Space

Resolution	16GB	32GB	64GB	128GB
8 megapixels	5722	11444	22888	45776
12 megapixels	3814	7629	15258	30516
16 megapixels	2861	5722	11444	22,888
22 megapixels	2080	4161	8322	16644

the amount of detail you need in the images with the amount of memory needed to store these images.

There are at least two dozen file formats that allow a digital camera to save an image. The type you will use depends on the type of image and how you anticipate using it. In Table 3.6, I show the most common digital image formats (JPEG, TIFF, GIF, RAW) and their primary uses and associated strengths and weaknesses.

The two most important (and interrelated) points to consider in determining file format are compression and archiving. Compression shrinks down the image file so it takes up less storage space, and some image formats compress better than others. Digital file formats that have high compression rates allow you to store more compressed images on a hard drive or external storage device.

JPEG (Joint Photographic Experts Group) files are the best file format for compression, since they can compress an image to between 1/10th to 1/20th of its original size. The exceptional compression rate for a JPEG image comes at a cost, however. The JPEG gets its high compression rate because it uses a "lossy compression" process that sacrifices detail. It tosses out redundant or closely redundant pixels from the image, never to be recovered again. In addition, repeatedly opening and closing a JPEG file results in degradation of the image quality. It is widely accepted that JPEG file formats should not be used for archiving images.

Image file formats that operate on a "lossless compression" (TIFF, GIF, and RAW) compress at a lower rate than images saved in a "lossy compression" format, reducing the file size by encoding the image information more efficiently, not by eliminating information. TIF (Tag Image File) and GIF (Graphic Interchange Format) compressed files can be shrunk down to about 50 percent of their original file sizes. You can save fewer lossless image files than lossy files on the same size hard drive; decompressed, the lossless files restore the photograph to its original condition with no information lost. As a result, TIFF files are currently considered the best image file formats for archiving digital images.

There is a handful of ways to capture digital images in the field. The three most widely applied types of digital cameras used by planners are: digital cameras,

Table 3.6 Applications, Strengths, and Weaknesses of Common Digital Image Formats

Common Format	Applications	Strengths	Weaknesses
JPEG	High-quality, full color image. Great for web and PowerPoint.	Large rate of compression (lossy compression)	Degeneration of image after repeated savings (loss compression)
TIFF	High-quality, full color image. Very effective for archiving and image editing.	Visual information is not lost after repeated openings of the file (lossless compression)	Low compression rate in comparison to JPEG (lossless compression)
GIFF	Lower quality full color, black and white, or line image. Only 256 colors.	a) Smaller file size than TIFF since it deals with a smaller spectrum of colors. b) Visual information is not lost after repeated openings of the file (lossless compression)	a) Smaller spectrum of colors b) Low compression rate in comparison to JPEG (lossless compression)
RAW	High-quality, full color image	Visual information is not lost after repeated openings of the file (lossless compression)	a) Format depend on camera manufacturer; rarely compatible with other image editing software packages b) Low compression rate in comparison to JPEG (lossless compression)

cellphones/tablets, and drones. Each type of digital camera comes with video capacity and has its own particular strengths and unique vistas that it provides the planner when conducting their photographic investigation. Digital cameras provide the greatest range of focal lengths and will provide you with the deepest range of megapixels per image (up to 50+ megapixels). With the benefits of extra detailed image quality, digital cameras come with extra girth and cost. All planning offices should have at least one high-quality digital camera to be used for long and medium range shot images for projects that require multiple vistas.

Smartphones (and to a lesser extent tablets as a function of their larger size) have changed how the world goes about photography. Smartphones change the way we execute digital images in three ways: mobility (your cellphone is always on hand), unlimited storage capacity (images can be stored on the cellphone service provider's cloud), and connectivity (real-time connectivity of sharing images via the internet). The most significant benefit to smartphones is that they are free (you already own a cellphone) and they allow you to capture "changes taking place in the blink of an eye". [19] The most dramatic drawback to smartphone images is the much smaller megapixels depth (around 8 megapixels) which limits the amount of detailed information recorded in the image.

Drone photography has become more widely accessible to planning researchers in the last five years. There are some very significant regulatory obligations that you need to meet before you begin your drone photographic investigation. Federal Aviation Administration (FAA) guidelines (Title 14 of the Code of Federal Regulations, Part 107) require that anyone operating a civil small unmanned aircraft system (sUAS) in the National Airspace System for applications other than hobby and recreation should hold a remote pilot-in-command (PIC) certification. All planners operating a drone for public or private purpose are required to be certified PICs and need to be insured for possible damages and injury as a result of an sUAS accident.

Using a drone for photographic applications is called Visual Reconnaissance Analysis (VRA). The most important value to drone images is that they provide aerial footage of the community that is real-time in relation to internet aerial images (e.g. Google Earth) that are updated once every two to three years (or longer in rural areas). A drone provides three distinct Mapping and Surveying elevation vistas: high elevation (400 feet), middle elevation (200 feet), and low elevation (100 feet). I recently applied a drone VRA in the study of Lamar, SC, as a part of a main street development plan and use images from this research to illustrate the applications of these three vistas. High elevation drone images were taken to show Main Street in relation to a larger perimeter. In Figure 3.12, it is clear that there are two Main Streets: a Northeast dense commercial corridor (right side of the street) and a Southwest significantly less density mixed-use corridor (left side of the street). Façade and storefront restoration will most likely take place on the Southside of the street while new developments will take place on the Northside of the street.

Middle elevation AVR images show the co-locations of buildings in relation to the street. The Lamar community has put in a tremendous amount of effort

Figure 3.12 Two Main Streets

Figure 3.13 Main Street Awnings

Figure 3.14 Site A on Main Street

to encourage Main Street businesses to invest in a standardized green awning system that makes the storefronts and sidewalks very inviting to pedestrian traffic. (See Figure 3.13.) As shown in this image, storefront awnings attract pedestrians by providing shelter from the sun.

Low elevation AVR images can show a tremendous amount of detailed information about a particular site that are literally invisible with Google Earth aerial images. In particular, low elevation AVR images can provide three-dimensional understanding (length, breadth, and depth) of place. Figure 3.14 is an image of a vacant Main Street lot that once was the location of a gas station. The image is able to show the space in relation to its immediate background of a brick wall and metal shed and behind that the fire station.

DISCUSSION QUESTIONS

1. How can a multidecade photographic analysis help with comprehensive planning and zoning?
2. Although "real-to-life" photographic research appears like that to the reader of research, can you see how it provides a little too simplified view of reality?

3. How would you organize your shooting guide to integrate multiple vistas of a particular topic? How would each particular vista (e.g. local view) relate to a different perspective on the topic? Lastly, can you see how to integrate different types of digital cameras (e.g. cellphone and drone) to capture different vistas?
4. Photographic research is a great way to document small incremental changes in the community. How would you organize a photographic research project to document the implementation of a new urban capital improvement project?

NOTE

i Portions of this discussion appeared in: Gaber, John, and Gaber, Sharon. 2004. "If you can see what I know: Moving planners' use of photographic images from illustration to empirical data," *Journal of Architectural and Planning Research*, 21(3), pp. 222–238; and Gaber, John. 1994. "Manhattan's 14th Street vendors' market: Informal street peddlers' complementary relationship with New York City's economy," *Urban Anthropology*, Winter, 23(4), pp. 373–408.

REFERENCES

[1] Collier, J., and Collier, M. 1990. *Visual Anthropology: Photography as a Research Method*. Albuquerque, NM: University of New Mexico Press, p. 19.
[2] Dandekar, H. (ed.). 2003. *The Planner's Use of Information*. Chicago, IL: Planners Press, pp. 299–301.
[3] Larsen, P. 1999. "Writing about photographs," in *Symbolic Imprints*, edited by L. Bertelsen, R. Gade, and M. Sandbye. Oakville: Aarhus University Press, p. 11; Scruton, R. 1981. "Photography and representation," *Critical Inquiry*, 7(3), p. 588.
[4] Collier and Collier, *Visual Anthropology*, p. 17.
[5] Riis, J. 1971. *How the Other Half Lives*. New York: Dover Publications, Inc.
[6] Collier and Collier, *Visual Anthropology*, p. 4.
[7] Collier and Collier, *Visual Anthropology*, p. 169.
[8] Gans, H. 1982. *The Urban Villagers*. New York: The Free Press.
[9] Collier and Collier, *Visual Anthropology*, pp. 182–183.
[10] Barrett, T. 1990. *Criticizing Photographs: An Introduction to Understanding Images*. Mountain View, CA: Mayfield Publishing Company, p. 35.
[11] Banks, M. 1998. "Visual anthropology: Image, object, and interpretations," in *Image-based Research: A Source Book for Qualitative Researchers*, edited by J. Prosser. London: Falmer Press, p. 10.
[12] Gaber, J., and Gaber, S. 2004. "If you can see what I know: Moving planners' use of photographic images from illustration to empirical data," *Journal of Architectural and Planning Research*, 21(3), p. 266.
[13] Snyder, J., and Allen, N.W. 1975. "Photography, vision, and representation," *Critical Inquiry*, 2(1), pp. 151–152.

[14] Collier and Collier, *Visual Anthropology*, p. 13; Prosser, J., and Schwarz, D. 1998. "Photographs within the sociological research process," in *Image-based Research: A Source Book for Qualitative Researchers*, edited by J. Prosser. London: Falmer Press, p. 119.

[15] Banks, "Visual anthropology," p. 10.

[16] Hicks, W. 1972. "What is photojournalism?" in *Photographic Communication*, edited by R.S. Schuneman. New York: Hastings House Publishers, p. 33.

[17] Forsyth, A. 1999. "Soundbite cities: Imaging futures in debates over urban form," *Journal of Architectural and Planning Research*, 16(1), p. 46.

[18] Gaber, J. 1994. "Manhattan's 14th Street vendors' market: Informal street peddlers' complementary relationship with New York City's economy," *Urban Anthropology*, Winter, 23(4), pp. 373–408, 380–381.

[19] Gaber, J. 2016. "Data everywhere: Qualitative research meets cellphones," *Knowledge Center* published post, American Planning Association website, 10/11.

4

FOCUS GROUP RESEARCH

WHAT IS FOCUS GROUP RESEARCH?

Focus group research is designed to gather spoken data from members of a small group. The individuals belong to a clearly defined geographic community (neighborhood) or shared interest group (such as park consumers) or more rarely, the general public (residents of the community).

A skilled group facilitator presents a series of questions in a conversational format. The comments are recorded and, later, analyzed. Focus group research always incorporates more than one focus group meeting. Planners will either conduct several group meetings with different recognizable communities to get a wider breadth of comments on a focused topic or hold several meetings from the same community to get a greater depth on a focused topic within the community.

WHY DO PLANNERS NEED FOCUS GROUP RESEARCH?

Planners decide on focus group research for a number of reasons. First, focus group research is an efficient and economical way to interview large numbers of people in the community. The same time and effort that it takes to interview one person can be used to interview several people in a focus group simultaneously. Focus groups also are a more welcoming way to interview members in the community; residents sit with a group, which helps allay some of the fears they may have about talking with planning researchers. Furthermore, focus group research implicitly, if not explicitly, empowers participants to talk to the planner because they outnumber her. In a typical focus group meeting, there are 8 to 10 participants and only one planner, acting as the facilitator.

Focus group research's major strength lies with the planner's ability to talk directly with the "data"—the members of the community. When you want detailed, qualitative data straight from the community's mouth, this is the method to choose. You can ask follow-up questions based on earlier comments; assess the intensity of residents' experiences by observing their body language and gauging the volume of their voices; cross-validate one resident's comments and experiences to another's; and play the "devil's advocate" role to test potential planning options and see how the residents react to various ideas.

Focus group research also provides you with an immediate impression of what is happening in the community. After completing a focus group session, you will have a rough sense of the more significant topics confronting the group. However, unlike survey research, where the investigator waits and analyzes all the completed surveys before learning the tenor of what's going on in the community, the conversational format of focus group data makes it easy for a planner to pick the most salient themes and hear the intensity of the reactions to those themes in the meeting.

WHEN DO PLANNERS USE FOCUS GROUP RESEARCH?

Planners use focus group research when they need more in-depth, qualitative data than can be obtained from a survey, but not the fine-grain detail that is generated from individual interviews. Focus group research helps a planner discover how a particular situation affects the various groups confronted by it. For example, changing the zoned density of an industrial land use may have different impacts on the immediate industrial businesses in comparison to neighboring residents. A focus group research strategy can be used to understand how the existing zoned land use currently affects the two groups and to gauge how the proposed zoning change may affect them.

Doing Focus Group Research

What makes focus group research appear deceptively easy is the short amount of time needed to do it and the somewhat enjoyable process of getting data through a series of meetings. Unfortunately, the meetings constitute only a fraction of the work involved in this research strategy. You will spend an extensive amount of time and effort in setting up the meetings and organizing and analyzing the data afterward. This effort makes focus group research a powerful qualitative tool.

Setting Up

To correctly set up a focus group meeting, you need to establish the research topics, determine the site location and what preparation is needed, get the right community to the meeting, and scope the size of the focus group investigation. Below, I discuss each of these tasks in more detail.

Establishing the Research Topics

Since focus group research involves a guided conversation with strangers, it is very easy for the focus of the meeting to stray off track. Therefore, it is important for you to have a firm understanding of what questions you need answered before stepping into the meeting. To establish the foundation of the focus group research, you need to address three questions. First, what do you need to learn by the end of the meeting? Remember, unlike a quantitative research strategy, observations obtained through focus group meetings will be more detailed and identify empirical nuances you never imagined before the research project started.

The second research question, and the one that planners tend to fail with the most, is: "Who or where is the community?" Conducting a brilliant focus group research project, but getting input from the wrong community, is a waste of time and resources. By wrong community, we mean individuals who either do not have personal experience related to the topic at hand or have not witnessed a situation related to the topic.

In this line of research, focus group participants are virtually your sole source of data. Many times, planners fail to recognize that several different communities need to participate. These tend to be either geographic differences (both sides of the street, upstream and downstream, suburban and rural) or different perspectives (industrial businesses and neighboring residents, residents of group homes and immediate neighbors, business owners and commuters), or a combination of the two.

Third, how much detail do you need from the research? The depth and breadth of the type of data generated depends on the organization of the interview guide. The planner who runs the meeting and guides the conversation is informed by this guide, which identifies all the questions that need to be addressed and at what point during the meeting. You can memorize these questions to make the focus group meeting appear more spontaneous, but we suggest you keep a copy close at hand, just in case.

Organize the questions in a logical, conversational progression and make sure the questions connect to each other either substantively (consecutive questions addressing the same topic) or intuitively (consecutive questions focusing on different research related topics, but allowing participants to see the connection). The way the questions are organized should encourage people to talk about topics central to the research project. To get people talking, start the meeting with easy, nonthreatening questions. Once everyone in the meeting is comfortable talking, ask the more difficult questions in the middle of the meeting. These questions tend to be the most important questions in the research project. Stick to a few questions so focus group participants do not feel inundated.

Depending on the research situation, I like to close out our focus group meetings with one of these types of questions: Very specific questions that narrow in on a specific topic discussed in the meeting; open-ended, "What if?" questions that let people talk about an idealized situation; or applications questions that test different possible planning scenarios to see how people think about the options as they relate to their day-to-day lives.

Second, phrase each question so people will be eager to talk. Of course, this is more challenging than it sounds, but two caveats can help you construct good focus group questions. First, make sure the question is worded so participants clearly understand it. Stay away from slang or technical terms (like GIS or NIMBY) and use words that people use in an everyday conversation. Also, phrase the questions in an open-ended way, so participants can be confident that their experiences relate to the topic and so they will want to contribute to the discussion. For example, a question like "Who here has been stuck in traffic on Main Street during rush hour?" tends to encourage interaction. This situation has likely been shared by every driver in town.

Meeting Location and Preparation

Since most focus group meetings tend to be held after work or on weekends, make sure the building and meeting room are easily accessible and safe so people will want to come. Bear in mind that buildings and places can be extremely politically charged environments. Pick locations that are fairly nondescript, familiar to participants, accessible, and easy to find. Hotels, schools, libraries, community centers, churches, and temples make good meeting places. How the meeting place is organized is equally important. Effective room preparation greatly promotes a positive first impression. Arrive at the room early to prepare it (think about the seating arrangement) and be there to welcome the participants.

Getting People to the Meeting

It is always a challenge to get people from the community to come to the meeting, to get the right people to participate in the meeting, and to get a good sample of the community. Focus groups bring together a group of strangers from a methodologically predefined "community." This said, it should be apparent that it isn't easy to get complete strangers to come to a focus group meeting where they will be asked to share their experiences in an orchestrated conversation that will impact a planning decision.

Give the community a significant amount of advance notice (at least one month) that you have scheduled a series of focus group meetings and need them to attend. Get the word out to the community about upcoming focus group meetings through door-to-door contacts, mail, phone calls, and posted announcements. Each approach has its own particular strengths and weaknesses in getting to the target community in terms of length of time, cost, and response rate. (See Table 4.1.)

The best way to get the word out to the targeted people in the community and have a high rate of attendance is by going door-to-door to talk to them about the upcoming focus group meetings. However, this approach is very costly in terms of both time and money.

The phone contact approach has become much less precise over the last 15 years with cellphones replacing landlines, but still can be very precise in targeting the identified community and having a high attendance success rate when you have an up-to-date phone list of community residents. It is less costly in terms of labor hours than the door-to-door approach because you can contact future focus group participants at your convenience from your office.

As precise as phone calls, but slightly less successful because it lacks a personal touch, is the mail approach. This approach suffers from the same weakness as the phone approach—not up-to-date addressees—and postage adds a little extra cost. However, the mail approach is much less time-consuming than the more labor-intensive door-to-door and phone approaches.

An offshoot to physical mail notices is using e-mail to post notifications. Although extremely cost-effective, this approach runs into the problem of missing members of the community who do not have an e-mail address. Also, e-mail addresses are not space-specific. Residents who keep their e-mail addresses after they move out of the community may be incorrectly notified about a focus group meeting, resulting in a compromise of the integrity of the identified community.

Table 4.1 Approaches to Informing the Community about Scheduled Focus Group Meetings

| Approach | Variables | | | |
	Precision	Time	Cost	Success Rate
Door-to-Door	Very precise. Word gets to targeted community.	Most time-consuming. Larger the community, more time needed to reach out to the community.	Most costly. Very high labor costs.	Most successful. Local residents like the in-person contact.
Phone	Precise with landlines, not precise with cellphones. Risks for landlines are missing people with unlisted numbers and getting a very skewed sample of the non-cellphone users population. Risks for cellphones are reaching former community residents who no longer live in the community.	Very time-consuming. It takes a good amount of time to call and talk with area residents.	Somewhat costly. High labor cost.	Hit-and-miss. Some planning research projects may lend themselves to landline populations. With caller ID, cellphone contacts are dependent on the community resident taking a call from your organization ("City of …").
Mail	Precise. Risks missing people with unlisted addresses.	Less time-consuming. Write the publication and mail.	Somewhat costly. Cost of postage and printed material.	Successful.
E-mail	Very precise if e-mail addresses are up-to-date.	Least time-consuming. Write the announcement and send via your computer.	Least costly.	Very successful.
Electronic Posted Announcement	Not precise. Researchers have no idea who sees the publication.	Least time-consuming. Write publication and post.	Least costly.	Hit-and-miss. Not sure who actually sees the posted announcement.

The least precise and lowest success rate for promoting attendance is the electronic posted announcement approach (on a city website or posted ad on a community website). Here, you have no control over who actually sees the announcement; it can be a member of the community or someone who is just passing through a series of neighborhood websites. With these weaknesses, however, come two great strengths: The posted announcement approach is cheap and takes very little time.

These notification approaches are not mutually exclusive. You can and should combine a couple of approaches to ensure greater visibility of the upcoming focus group meetings. For example, you may want to start your campaign to recruit the community with a mail announcement and then follow up with a phone call.

HOW MANY FOCUS GROUPS ARE ENOUGH?

When do you know you have conducted enough focus group meetings? Planning and public policy researchers tend to answer this question differently than nonpolicy researchers, such as marketers. Nonpolicy researchers use focus groups with the primary goal of saturation to determine the number of focus group meetings they hold. Saturation in focus group research is the duplication of observations—no one is saying anything new—in subsequent meetings. Within this context, the rule of thumb of "three to four groups with any one type of participant" is considered sufficient. [1] It is with saturation (participants in different focus group meetings making similar observations) that nonpolicy focus group researchers obtain "confidence" that their research has generated a representative understanding of an identified population on how it thinks about a particular topic.

Planners push the envelope of focus group research because they strive to get both a saturation of observations and the best representative sample (within budgetary reason) of the community. For planners, saturation in focus group research occurs when they get duplicating observations, and they are confident that what was observed in the meetings is representative of the community they are researching. What is considered "representative" of the community depends on what type of focus group research strategy the planner is pursuing.

There are two types of focus group research strategies that planners can use: Intensive and comprehensive. In *intensive* focus group research, you will work with a small community (roughly 100 individuals or less) and try to get a saturation of observations with a representative number of individuals from the community. Intensive focus group research uses a purposeful recruiting process where everyone in the community is known and everyone is asked to participate in the meetings. In this case, 60 percent participation or more is a good representation of the community. The higher the number of people participating in the focus group meetings, the higher the confidence you will have that your qualitative research findings are representative of the entire community.

By contrast, a comprehensive focus group research strategy is a large-scale research project having a community population in the range of hundreds to thousands of people. Given the large numbers of individuals, the recruiting process for participants looks dramatically different. This research starts with a random sampling procedure since it is dealing with a large population. In a random sample, everyone in the community has the same probability of being included in the research project. The percent of confidence can be estimated to determine the number of individuals and the number of meetings needed to achieve a desired rate of confidence. As shown in Table 4.2, in a random sample, a 95 percent confidence level with + or - 10 percent sampling error and 50/50 split, it is not out of the question to have a fairly representative sample of a community with 50,000 to 100,000 people. For example, with a population

Table 4.2 Sample Size for the 95 Percent Confidence Interval

Population Size	± 3 percent Sampling Error		± 5 percent Sampling Error		± 10 percent Sampling Error	
	50/50 split	80/20 split	50/50 split	80/20 split	50/50 split	80/20 split
100	92	87	80	71	49	38
250	203	183	152	124	70	49
500	341	289	217	165	81	55
750	441	358	254	185	85	57
1,000	516	406	278	198	88	58
2,500	748	537	333	224	93	60
5,000	880	601	357	234	94	61
10,000	964	639	370	240	95	61
25,000	1,023	665	378	245	96	61
50,000	1,045	674	381	245	96	61
100,000	1,056	678	383	245	96	61
1,000,000	1,066	682	384	246	96	61
100,000,000	1,067	683	384	246	96	61

Source: Salant, Priscilla, and Dillman, Don. 1994. How to Conduct Your Own Survey. New York: John Wiley & Sons, Inc, p. 55.

of 50,000 people, you can conduct 10 focus group meetings with a random sample of at least 10 individuals each to get a roughly 95 percent confidence level at a 50/50 split that your focus group observations are fairly representative of the community.

How to read this table: First, look at the population size on the left side of the table. If your population is a neighborhood of 400 people, use the 500 population. Select the population into which your population fits. If you are a planner for New York City, use the 100,000,000 population, because the city's population is larger than 1,000,000. Next, determine the level of sampling error that you can tolerate. Typically, in social sciences a ± 5 percent sampling error is acceptable. If you need or feel more comfortable with less error use the 3 percent and if you can tolerate greater error you can use the 10 percent rate. Finally, you have to determine whether your population is homogeneous (or "like-minded") about the planning issue under investigation or whether the population is heterogeneous or of diverse perspectives about the issue. As the sample size indicates, if a population is of diverse perspectives (you use the 50/50 split) then you need a larger sample to adequately capture the full range of views. If you do not know what to expect from the group, and cannot anticipate whether they are similar or diverse, use the diverse (50/50) split rate to enhance the validity of the sample.

A stakeholder engagement is a large-scale research technique that looks similar to a comprehensive focus group research project, but lacks the methodological rigor of a focus group investigation. Stakeholder engagement projects are usually a two-hour meeting that purposefully integrates multiple and many times contradictory community perspectives in a single session to generate a holistic snapshot of the "community's perspective." This is in contrast to focus group investigations that are looking to isolate a particular community perspective. Consequently, stakeholder engagement projects lack reliability in that each stakeholder meeting can and will dramatically yield different take-aways, making it difficult for the planner to isolate "the community's perspective" to specific populations in the community. In Chapter 7 I provide a detailed discussion on how stakeholder engagement and key informant investigations are used in citizen participation projects.

The Size of the Group

Having confidence that focus group observations adequately represent the community when they either have significant representation of the entire community (intensive focus group research) or a representative random sample (comprehensive focus group research) is only half of the focus group confidence equation.

The other half involves the number of individuals who participate in each focus group meeting. The standard range for an acceptable number of focus group participants falls between 6 and 12 individuals per meeting. There is a give-and-take relationship between the number of focus group participants and the amount of confidence the researchers have that the focus group meeting generated an accurate portrait of what is going on in the community: As the number of focus group participants increases, the amount of confidence the researchers have in the focus group meeting's ability to generate accurate observations decreases. More specifically, as the focus group size increases, the number of opportunities and the amount of time participants have to share their experiences decreases.

However, the inverse relationship between group size and confidence does not hold true. Extremely small focus group meetings with two or three people do not increase confidence in the value of the focus group observations. Too small a number tends to increase the likelihood of one person dominating the meeting and runs the risk of the conversation getting thin, with too little to talk about.

The best way to gauge the ideal focus group size is to judge the complexity of the topics to be discussed. (See Figure 4.1.) More complex focus group topics do better with a smaller number of participants (5 to 8 people) because they require more time for participants to reflect and share their experiences. Simpler focus group topics can succeed with a larger group (9 to 12 participants) because their experiences are more immediate, and they can more concisely share their observations in the meeting.

LARGE NUMBER OF PARTICIPANTS

(+) more people talking
(-) people may not want to
  talk in front of a large
  group of people
	20+
	19
	18
	17
	16
	15
	14
	13
	12
	11
		(+) more people talking
		(-) may lose people
		(-) not enough time to talk
		(-) people may not want to
		  talk in front of a large
		  group of people

SIMPLE TOPIC
 	
(+) people have plenty of
  time to talk
(-) conversation may get thin
(-) 1 or 2 people may
  dominate conversation
	10
	9
	8
	7
	6
	5
	4
	3
		COMPLEX TOPIC
		
		(+) fewer people allow more
		  time to talk
		(-) conversation may get thin
		(-) 1 or 2 people may
		  dominate conversation

SMALL NUMBER OF PARTICIPANTS

Figure 4.1 Relationship of Focus Group Size to Focus Group Topic

Usually you will end up with larger-than-optimum-sized focus group meetings, for several reasons. In general, planners tend to work with large populations, tend to present research questions that are part of a politically charged topic in the community (leading to increased participation), and tend not to discourage attendance. After all, it is politically unwise to tell people who made the effort to attend the meeting that they are not needed that day and to come back another time. Those people most likely will not be able to attend another day. Unlike nonpolicy focus group researchers, who can compensate would-be focus group members if they are not needed for a particular meeting, the focus group researcher does not have such a luxury and must include everyone who shows up.

Managing the Meeting

What is the best way to manage large focus group meetings? If possible, break up large groups into smaller ones and run simultaneous focus group meetings. If this is not feasible, you will need to figure out how to manage the meeting. When confronted with a larger focus group meeting (more than 12 to 18 participants), modify the process and incorporate "nominal group" techniques to ensure that everyone at the meeting is able to share individual observations.

The nominal group technique is a specific type of group interviewing process that focuses on making sure everyone in the group is able to provide non-overlapping experiences and observations in the meeting. [2] Incorporating these techniques to manage large focus group meetings will bolster your confidence that everyone in the meeting is heard and that their opinions are recorded.

The observations raised in the large focus group meetings are still compromised because of the large number of participants. This usually means less detailed comments (several sentences per participant) and shorter, less-detailed comments (one or two sentences per participant). It is important that the observations made from these large focus group meetings be noted along with other, regular-sized focus group meeting observations to account for the possible variances in the details of participant observations made among all focus group meetings. From our experience, observations generated in the large modified nominal group meetings tend to mirror the topics of observations made in the smaller focus group meetings, though they lack the depth of detail.

The nominal group strategy we most commonly apply in large focus group meetings is called the "snowball technique." [3] This technique allows everyone in attendance to provide their observations and have them recorded. After the initial introductions, each member of the focus group is handed two to three 4″ × 6″ cards and asked to write down observations about specific questions put forward by the focus group moderator. Afterwards, the cards are taped to a wall so everyone in the meeting can see the various observations, although they don't know who wrote them. The cards are then arranged into shared themes by the focus group facilitator (it is helpful to have one in this situation). Members of the group discuss each one, starting with the largest themes (those with the most cards) to the smallest. The snowball discussion then moves to the other questions identified in the interview guide. At the very least, the snowball technique allows everyone an opportunity to share personal observations and have them discussed by the group.

Recording the Data

To get the qualitative data you need, you must record people's observations about what they have experienced or witnessed, as well as their opinions on why things happened the way they did. These observations, stories, or what Rubin and Rubin [4] call "narratives"—where people describe what happened in a simple straightforward way with little elaboration—are what planning researchers search for in focus group meetings. Interpretations on why things happen can provide insights about factors you have not previously recognized.

Two standard methods of recording these observations are written notes and digital recordings. Handwritten notes are very dependable because they do not require batteries and never suffer from mechanical malfunctions. However, note taking is very unreliable because of a high margin of error: the note taker may not be able to capture everything said in the meeting. Also, written notes miss the nuances of volume and pronunciation. Because of these weaknesses, making an audio recording of focus group meetings is the best way to accurately capture what was said and how it was said. Digital recording is the current technological evolution of this technique. These devices are a huge improvement over tape recorders, which are bulky and cumbersome to operate.

Organizing the Data

After each session, you organize the data that have been collected, translating recorded comments into electronic text and onto paper. Krueger and Casey [5] identify two ways to transcribe focus group meetings: transcript-based and tape-based abridged transcript. Transcript-based data organization provides a word-for-word transcription of the entire conversation. This is a time-intensive process that takes hours. Conservative estimates [6] put the transcription time of a two-hour focus group meeting at 8 to 12 hours! In the past, this very fact has made focus group research impractical for time-pressed planners.

Tape-based (the name remains although the machines today are mostly digital) abridged transcription is much less time-consuming. [7] In this process, you listen to the recorded focus group meeting and transcribe only the relevant portions of the conversation. More often than not, we use this method for transcribing focus group meetings. We found that a two-hour focus group meeting takes roughly one to four hours to transcribe this way.

During the transcription process, keep in mind how you want to organize the data. In fact, think of the interview guide as a chronological filing cabinet during the data organization stage of the research process. Assuming the focus group conversation went according to plan and loosely followed the interview guide, comments made in the focus group meeting can be sequentially organized per interview guide question. Make sure to insert any significant observations that were an offshoot of the original question. Many times these unanticipated observations provide new and interesting insights.

After each focus group session is transcribed into separate files, you will electronically stitch them together per question. This way you will cut and paste all the observations from each focus group meeting and their offshoot observations into a cumulative pool of observations by question, following the entire interview guide throughout. At the end of the data organization process, you should have a file of observations from each focus group session and a cumulative file of all the observations from each of the different focus group meetings as they relate to each interview guide question.

Analyzing the Data

One of the illuminating characteristics of focus group research is how all the observations generated in separate focus group meetings come together into a single, rich, and detailed data set. I use *content analysis* (see Chapter 5 for more details on this method) in two ways: top-down, using the interview guide as a sieve to read through the focus group comments, or bottom-up (grounded), looking at key words used in the meetings or types of participants who participated in the meetings (for example, a stay-at-home mom or daily commuter) to evaluate the focus group comments. An interview guide analysis looks at the focus group comments according to the specific topics brought up in the conversations, as prompted by the interview guide.

When conducting a content analysis, look for both manifest (quantitative) and latent (qualitative) data characteristics. A *manifest content analysis* (in content analysis language, this is also called "vote counting") looks at the number of participant comments that cluster around shared themes. If a high number of comments surround a specific topic, you know this item is important to the group. For example, in a hypothetical downtown parking focus group study, we find the highest concentration of comments around the topic of "finding downtown parking." In a manifest analysis of focus group data, comments can be hierarchically organized in terms of higher number or lower number of comments made around specific topics.

However, a high density of comments around a specific topic does not mean a convergence (agreement) of comments. If you assume this, you run the risk of oversimplifying the fine-grain details raised in the meetings. The clustering of focus group comments can include divergent observations. For example, in looking at the density of comments around "finding downtown parking," some participants discuss the difficulty in finding parking while others report little difficulty. The two observations share the topic but make two different sets of conclusions.

Analyzing topical focus group data according to a *latent content analysis* involves looking at focus group comments for links between variables. Going back to the downtown parking focus groups example, let's say you learn that there is a clustering of comments around parking strategies. A closer investigation of these comments shows that some people have a hard time finding parking while others have little difficulty. Sifting through these comments and looking for connections, you learn why there is a difference between the two parking experiences. Among those commuters who have difficulty finding parking, there are some who tend to look for parking spaces close to their workplaces and leave for work during peak rush-hour traffic. On the other hand, those commuters who have less difficulty finding parking fall into two subcategories: those who leave for work before the rush hour traffic, and those who look for parking that is not as close to where they work.

QUESTIONS OF VALIDITY AND RELIABILITY IN FOCUS GROUP RESEARCH

You should anticipate potential challenges to validity and reliability in your focus group research findings. You will usually have a harder time answering questions of internal validity than those dealing with external validity, such as whether you improperly applied observations from one project to another situation. This is because focus group research is most commonly applied to very specific planning questions, making it highly unlikely for any similar situations to be comparable.

You run the risk of failing to answer the question of internal validity in three ways. (See Table 4.3.) The first is by not getting a representative sample of community participants. This very significant problem can be difficult to overcome, but you can protect yourself. First, get a statistical census of who is in the community. For a neighborhood focus group research project, census tract data for the

Table 4.3 Most Common Questions of Internal Validity in Focus Group Research

	Type of Question	Problem	Evidence Reached	Solution
1. Sampling	A. Not a numeric representative sample	Unrepresentative numeric sample of the community	Low numbers of people attending focus group meetings	Get a total population of the research community, then figure how many more members of the community need to attend to make the sample viable
	B. Not a representative sample	Focus group sample does not resemble community profile	Attendees don't represent topic being researched	a) Change focus group meeting dates and times b) Purposefully sample target populations
2. Moderator Bias	A. Facilitator domination	Facilitator dominates the conversation	Transcripts show too many facilitator comments and too few community comments	a) Change facilitators b) Facilitator adjusts meeting behavior
	B. Facilitator verbal bias	Facilitator provides unfair positive and negative comments	Transcripts show facilitator's positive and negative comments	a) Change facilitators b) Facilitator adjusts meeting behavior
3. Interpretation	A. Incorrect reading of the observations	Improper reading of transcripts	a) Under-and over-valuing comments b) Misread comments	a) Vote counting b) Direct quotes of comments

area will give you a good picture of who lives in the neighborhood by gender, ethnicity, income level, and home ownership.

By comparing the census data image of the neighborhood to the characteristics of the focus group participants, you can determine how representative your focus group participants are of the actual neighborhood as a whole. Therefore, it is very important to keep track of who participated in the meetings by respondent characteristics (gender, zip code, age, etc.) to be able to answer this question of internal validity.

If the focus group research sample is done with businesses or a specific business district, it is important to get a representative sample of all the different types of businesses in the area. This requires getting a census of the number of businesses in the identified community by type, size, and location to use as a benchmark for comparing the businesses represented in the focus group meetings.

Sometimes you will be confronted with focus group members who are not a representative sample of the community. As a solution, you can conduct more focus group meetings and specifically target those subpopulations missing in the first round. This alternative requires you to either change the time or place of the focus group meetings, or the method of recruiting participants—you may need to change from an announcement recruiting strategy to a more intensive approach, like door-to-door recruiting.

Another way planners may fail to address the question of internal validity lies with moderator bias during the meetings. This is when the moderator encourages specific observations that are not representative of the community as a whole. As you talk with community members, be mindful not to jeopardize the data as people share their experiences. Moderators can compromise participant responses by dominating the discussion or by biasing the participants' contribution to the conversation. More detail on these common moderator mistakes will help explain these shortfalls.

Moderator domination is an easy trap. If you talk too much, community members have little time to add their comments and discuss the topics. Traditional nonpolicy focus group meetings usually rely on skilled moderators who are very unlikely to have any expertise regarding the meeting topic. However, because you *are* well informed about the topic, you may easily go into too much detail while explaining the context of a question or asking a follow-up question to a participant's observation. Once the focus group participants get a sense that you are a good source of information, they may turn the tables and start asking *you* for answers to their questions. This is highly likely when the focus group research topic is politically charged and the community is desperately looking for the latest bit of information on the situation. Remember that every word you utter as the focus group moderator is another word not spoken by someone in the group. Keep in mind that the quality of focus group data is determined, in part, by the detail ("thick description") the community participants provide in their narratives.

There will always be moderator bias in focus group research. This fact is inescapable because the moderator engages in a conversational relationship with the focus group participant. Accept this intrinsic limitation but work hard to minimize it. The way you verbally respond to what people say can channel the direction of the conversation toward a nonrepresentative consensus, as well as amplify some voices in the meeting at the expense of others.

There are two types of verbal moderator bias—topical and nontopical. *Topical verbal bias* occurs when you provide too much positive verbal reinforcement to a participant's comments when they support an observation you like, or provide too little to comments that you do not like. *Nontopical moderator verbal bias* occurs when you provide too much positive verbal reinforcement toward participants with whom you personally most identify (men or business professionals, for example) and too little to others.

Finally, focus group data are vulnerable to threats of internal validity if you incorrectly interpret the focus group observations. You may mistakenly undervalue significant, widely shared observations, or overvalue underrepresented, uncommon observations, or outright misinterpret what people said in the meetings. You can avoid this through detailed documentation in your final report. When writing your focus group analysis, identify which observations were widely shared and discussed and set them apart from observations voiced by a minority of participants. Provide a few direct quotes from the focus group sessions as evidence that what you report is representative of what was said in the meetings.

External Validity

Unlike issues of internal validity, questions of external validity are very hard to avoid in focus group research. These questions can arise depending on how much you try to generalize from your representative focus group sample to explain other situations and populations. The challenge arises because the open conversational format, combined with the personal impact of the focus group sessions, can dramatically affect how you think about an entire host of activities. Powerful side comments, anecdotal stories, and little snippets about what happened to a focus group participant may have little to do with the primary issue of the meeting, but may tangentially connect to the topic and cause you to pause and think differently about related issues.

For example, in the Nebraska transit study discussed in greater detail in the following section, we focused on the needs of the transit disadvantaged, including the elderly, people too young to drive, the disabled, and low-income residents. Some of the comments made by the elderly transit disadvantaged in the Kearney focus meeting highlighted some very pointed issues regarding the general needs of the elderly in that community. As much as we wanted to comment about the overall needs of the elderly in Kearney, we could not; our focus group study focused on transit issues that included the elderly among other populations. It was not a study on the elderly that included transit issues. Since the focus group sample was representative of all the transit disadvantaged in Kearney and not just the elderly population, we could not generalize observations, no matter how true or telling they were about the elderly, for risk of violating questions of external validity.

Reliability

The question of reliability in focus group research looks at the ability of this research approach when replicated by a different researcher to come up with the same results. More specifically, it asks whether each focus group meeting was conducted in a standard process that allows separate focus group sessions to be combined into one data set. Some minor variability will occur among the different focus group meetings. For example, some meetings are held at night, while other meetings are held during the day; some meetings have five participants, while other meetings have 10.

The question of variability in focus group research looks at major changes in the execution of the research. Examples include changing the interview guide for each focus group meeting; changing the target population midway through the research project; or varying the focus group sizes widely (some meetings have only three participants while others have as many as 75). These wide variances affect your ability to compare the observations generated in one focus group meeting to observations made from another meeting even though they are part of the same study.

CASE STUDY #1: WIDENING EAST O STREET IN LINCOLN, NEBRASKA

This case study illustrates how I worked with a team of researchers that used an intensive focus group research strategy to get local business community input on a proposed street widening project for East O Street in Lincoln, Nebraska.

We were brought into the controversial project to learn why local businesses so adamantly opposed this change, while the city and its traffic engineers thought improving East O Street would help the very people who were opposing it. It is a story about how city officials made a proposed project more controversial than it needed to be because they failed to listen to the empirical data spoken to them by the community.

O Street is the main east–west thoroughfare that literally splits Lincoln into north and south sections. Growth had resulted in more traffic congestion on the city's primary thoroughfares. O Street has been a particular flash point of discussion and frustration for area residents. Between 52nd and 70th streets, O Street saw some of the heaviest traffic congestion in the city largely because of an intense concentration of commercial businesses, including a large indoor mall and several strip malls.

The City of Lincoln contracted with a local traffic engineering firm for an environmental assessment (EA) to determine if street improvements were needed and, if so, to identify roadway design options that could resolve the traffic congestion. The traffic engineers concluded that East O Street improvements were necessary to accommodate increasing traffic volumes. Their two specific roadway design recommendations were to widen the street from four to six lanes and to eliminate most of the curb cuts and left-hand turns. The consultants believed that the overall impacts to the community and neighborhood would be "minor," with a small caveat. They did recognize that traffic-sensitive businesses (like fast-food restaurants and drive-in banks) might be more adversely affected by relocations or changes in access. [8] However, these sacrifices were considered worthwhile in light of the benefits anticipated in vehicle and traffic safety and volume. [9] The proposed project was estimated at $15.2 million. Lincoln was able to get four-fifths of the proposed project federally funded; the mall was to pay $1.25 million and city funds were to pay the remainder. [10]

For 11 months after the proposed project went to the city council for a vote, officials were deadlocked on the proposed street-widening project because there was no majority support. Community resistance arose when both business owners and residents felt "betrayed" that their comments during the citizen participation phase in the EA were not integrated into the proposed project. [11] Additionally, the "business representatives complained they would lose access to streets under (the proposed) plans." [12] Adding to the intensity of the controversial project, the federal funds would evaporate if they were not encumbered for the project within a two-month period. The mayor, city council, and the chamber of commerce all wanted the project to be implemented for traffic congestion and economic reasons, such as adding more jobs to the local economy.

The chamber of commerce contracted us to run a trial meeting to determine if the local businesses and the public works department would be willing to try a focus group approach. An "issue identification" meeting was held with the East O Street business community, the traffic engineering consulting firm, the director of public works, and members of the city council. The vice president of government affairs for the Lincoln Chamber of Commerce attended the meeting as a witness to the assessment process.

Using the snowball technique, business representatives identified their top two concerns about the project. The concerns, listed in order of frequency, included a loss of access to East O Street, the resulting loss of business, the confusing system of streets feeding into East O Street (56th Street and Cotner Boulevard), and a loss of parking.

Impressed with the civility of business representatives' exchanges in the meeting, the director of public works, in a move unanticipated by the facilitators, closed the meeting, saying he supported this different way of citizen input. He would have the city's traffic engineers work closely with the business community to develop new design proposals for East O Street. It was now up to the planning consultants (us), working closely with the chamber of commerce, department of public works, and the city council, to make the process work and produce a final recommendation for the city council within the two-month period.

Geographically, the East O Street businesses were divided into seven blocks. It was assumed that businesses owners who occupy roughly the same geographic location on the street would share similar observations, experiences, and views about the project, making the meetings more focused. The chamber and the facilitators arranged a total of seven focus group meetings (one for each block) in a three-week period. We invited a total of 54 businesses to the meetings, and 35 (64.8 percent) of them attended. Each meeting was recorded; 900 minutes of discussions were transcribed and analyzed.

Our primary research goal was to hear from as many business owners as possible to learn how their businesses related to East O Street. We used a modified intensive focus group research approach that incorporated a nominal group technique. The meetings were held in a meeting room at a conveniently located O Street hotel and we supplied participants with city roadway maps and individual lot maps. Our approach was to start the meetings with a nominal group technique; we asked that each business owner describe how his business operated, including the way customers accessed the business from O Street. This initial format allowed the business owners to have the maximum individual input with no interruptions or interpretations from others. After each participant had a turn, the meeting opened for discussion so everyone could explore roadway or parking solutions.

What happened with daVinci's restaurant gives one example of how the focus group meetings went for most of the businesses. DaVinci's is an Italian restaurant located just off the northeast corner of 66th Street and O Street. The proposal designed a raised median along 66th Street to prevent traffic from going across it—this location had been the site of several traffic accidents involving cars turning left from O Street. According to the manager of daVinci's,

> Our main entrance is on 66th Street. ... Coming from the north on 66th Street, customers are going to have to turn in a half-mile [the closest curb cut allowing customers to access the restaurant from 66th Street] before the time they get to where I am at. By the time they see me, they are going to keep driving past me.

Then the manager of daVinci's, the city traffic engineer, and the focus group facilitators looked at the city map and the proposed median. Through their conversations, a collective idea arose to modify it. The change would allow people traveling south on 66th Street to turn into daVinci's, but prevent people from turning left out of the restaurant's driveway. The manager thought the left in, right out option "would help me out a ton." The city engineer said the proposed modification was worth taking a look at and analyzing in light of the rest of the project. In the end, the left in, right out option was incorporated in the final design.

At the end of all the meetings, most of the businesses were satisfied with the adjustments made to the East O Street proposal. The department of public works engineers worked closely with the consulting engineers and the local businesses to develop mitigating measures to offset many of the economic impacts of the proposed project. However, not all of the businesses impacted by the proposed East O Street project walked away from the focus group meetings completely satisfied with the outcome. Some felt that dividing the East O Street businesses into blocks was a way "to divide and conquer" the collective voice of the local businesses. Interestingly, this sentiment was mentioned only by a small number of merchants who did not participate in the small group meetings, and was voiced only at city council hearings covered by the local TV news.

We presented our focus group report to the city council in a precouncil meeting. Based on the series of focus group meetings, we found that, once the city engineers understood the particular problem each business owner had with the proposed project, simple mitigating measures could be incorporated easily into the new roadway design. These measures did not dramatically increase the cost of the project nor lessen the proposed traffic impact. That afternoon, the city council approved the East O Street project and adopted all the design recommendations defined by the planning researchers with a 6–1 vote. The city council was applauded in the local paper as doing "the right thing." The Lincoln *Journal Star* heralded the focus group meetings as "invaluable in clearing up some misconceptions on the part of property owners. They also produced some fine-tuning on the project itself." [13]

CASE STUDY #2: TRANSIT NEEDS ASSESSMENT IN MID-SIZED NEBRASKA COMMUNITIES

Many times, planners want to get spoken qualitative data slices from a large population, but they realize that it is too costly to do personal interviews or attempt an intensive focus group research approach. Comprehensive focus group research, combined with other quantitative and qualitative research, can help you get an understanding of a more complicated situation.

This case study is an example of using comprehensive focus group research within a larger research project designed to learn more about the transit disadvantaged in medium-sized Nebraska communities. Transit planners have always had a hard time assessing the needs of the transit disadvantaged consumers of public transportation. This challenge results in part because many of their needs are best identified by qualitative data (for example, wider steps on a bus) that are not easily quantifiable. [14]

Unfortunately, most of what transit planners look at to determine the need for transit services among the disadvantaged are numbers—the number of people aged 65 and older, the number of households with no vehicles available to them, the number of people living below the poverty line, and the number of people with mobility limitations.

Many transit disadvantaged residents felt they were ignored by the transit needs assessment Nebraska conducted in the mid-'90s. In 1993, the state completed an urban transit study of its two largest cities, Lincoln and Omaha. The counties these cities are in account for roughly 2 percent of Nebraska's land area, yet they have nearly 50 percent of the state's total population. The urban study was followed in 1995 by a rural and small town transit study meant to cover the rest of the state's transit needs.

Immediately after the completion of the nonurban transit study, residents from medium-sized communities voiced concern to the Nebraska State Department of Roads (NDOR) because they felt transit needs were not accurately reflected in the

1995 study. In 1996, NDOR contracted myself and a colleague to take a closer look at what they called the "perceived transit needs in mid-sized communities."

The goal of this study was to generate an overall assessment of transit needs in mid-sized Nebraska cities, which NDOR defined as those with a population between 8,000 and 50,000 that are not suburban communities of metropolitan areas (Lincoln and Omaha). We took a mixed method research approach that combined quantitative data (assessment of the numeric size of the transit disadvantaged populations in the 13 communities) and qualitative data (content analysis of transit needs assessment strategies, interviews with paratransit providers in the 13 communities, and three focus group meetings).

Because of limited funding, we found it impractical to conduct focus group meetings in all 13 communities; the driving time alone between our research base in Lincoln to the other communities ranged from two to seven hours each way. Instead, we divided the state into three sections (east, west, and central) and identified a medium-sized community located in each region of the state. Since we were unable to get a representative sample of all the medium-sized communities in the state, we adjusted the degree of how much impact the focus group could contribute to the overall research project. We thought the goal was still reasonable, despite the sampling limitations. We assumed the observations generated in the three group meetings could not be generalized for all 13 communities in the study, but we also thought the focus group data could help us better understand our transit demand quantitative data and our qualitative interview data from the 13 transit providers.

Recruiting meeting participants made an already logistically difficult focus group research project that much more challenging. We were faced with two immediate challenges: how to recruit participants who were so far away from the actual meeting places (we were a six-hour drive from the meeting location), and how to get a population that already lacks resources and physical mobility to attend the meetings. Our only option was a posted announcement recruiting strategy, designed to get the word out to the community members about the upcoming focus group meetings in their towns. We asked transit providers to post notices in their vehicles and to place a notice in each local paper, instructing participants who were interested in the focus group meetings to contact them. Each transit provider was instructed that no more than 20 participants could be invited to each focus group meeting and that these sessions were not "public meetings," but actually research meetings. Because the posted announcement strategy can be either very successful and recruit too many people or be very unsuccessful and result in only two to three people showing up (or no one at all!), we prestructured the focus group meetings to handle both large and small groups.

To ensure that transit-disadvantaged riders made it to the focus group meetings, we held the meetings at places they typically visited during the week—a community center, a senior center, and a centrally located church—and at times they were least likely to have schedule conflicts. We chose to have the meetings close to lunchtime so as not to conflict with doctor appointments or work.

Finally, we asked all transit riders who planned to attend the focus group meetings to schedule their rides to the meeting with the local transit service. All the transit service providers in the three communities provide mostly a nonfixed-route paratransit service. Patrons of the service commonly called it the "handi-bus," referring to small buses or vans that are handicapped accessible. Not so surprisingly, more than 95 percent of all people who participated in the focus group meetings rode the local handi-bus.

We were surprised to find common transit needs and themes in all three communities. More to what we expected, we found a handful of problems that were unique to the representative community. Each focus group meeting lasted two hours, resulting in 360 minutes of transcribed observations. What follows is an overview of what we found.

Scottsbluff/Gering

The City of Scottsbluff and its sister city, Gering, have a combined population of 22,028 and are located in Scotts Bluff County, which had a population of 37,161 at the time we conducted the focus group. The county is located in the western section of Nebraska, 15 miles from Wyoming. The neighboring cities are serviced by the Scotts Bluff County Handi-Bus, a demand-response transit service made up of nine vehicles, including five station wagons and four vans. The local service operates Monday through Friday, 8:00 a.m. to 4:30 p.m. and the elderly and disabled are charged significantly less per one-way ride compared to the general public, who pay up to three times as much as subsidized riders.

As we anticipated, the focus group meeting had too many people show up to the session. A total of 43 people were waiting for us in the local community center when we arrived. We were forced to make the meeting work. All were transit-disadvantaged and did not have the ability to go home and come back another day. Further, we had just driven many hours to conduct the meeting and were not scheduled or budgeted to do another focus group meeting in the area. We started the focus group meeting with a snowball nominal group technique to make sure everyone in the meeting at least had his/her observations recorded and analyzed.

It was widely accepted by all the participants that the handi-bus service helped the transit disadvantaged get around. One elderly woman said, "I have no family here, but I can depend on the handi-bus to take me to the doctor." The focus group participants identified four concerns in the meeting: the lack of late afternoon service, the fact that the steps on the buses were too high for some riders, the high cost for children to ride with disabled passengers, and the limited area the service covered.

Interestingly, when the focus group respondents were asked to rank their needs, the senior respondents ranked their needs differently from nonsenior respondents. Seniors picked time of service as their most pressing need, while nonseniors ranked access for kids and affordability as their priorities.

Norfolk

Norfolk, located in the northeast section of Nebraska, had a total population of 22,435 at the time of the study and is serviced by the Norfolk Handi-Bus, which provides a demand-response service within the city limits and operates two vehicles (one serves as a backup). A customer must request a ride 24 hours in advance and must schedule the trip between the hours of 7:00 a.m. to noon and 12:45 p.m. to 4:00 p.m., Monday through Friday. The elderly and disabled who use the service are charged half of what the general public pays.

The Norfolk focus group had 16 participants, more than anticipated but not an unmanageable number. The meeting was held shortly after lunch at the Norfolk Senior Center. About a third of the participants were not seniors, but saw the focus group announcement in the local paper and decided to participate. These nonriders provided an insight into the Norfolk Handi-Bus system we had not anticipated. This insight became apparent in our recording of the focus group meeting.

As with the Scottsbluff/Gering focus group, Norfolk participants identified the same benefits from the handi-bus and experienced similar problems. All of the participants shared personal stories about how the local transit service played an important role in their lives. One visually impaired elderly woman told her story like this: "I need it so I can be more independent. The last thing I want is to be in a nursing home."

The Norfolk participants identified four concerns regarding the local service: the limited hours of operation, especially the lack of lunchtime service; the need for more vehicles on busy travel days (Thursday and Friday); the need for weekend services; and the need for transit services for "other" people in the community—those who are not elderly, disabled, or in poverty. This last concern was strongly held by all of the participants who were neither elderly nor disabled. One working mother said: "I think the elderly['s] needs are taken care of. The problem is with getting to jobs. There is no focus on the other transit needs."

Kearney

Kearney is located in south-central Nebraska along Interstate 80. At the time of the focus group, Kearney had a population of 26,216 in a county of 39,516 residents. The community is served by the Senlow Transportation System, a nonfixed-route service with nine vehicles. (The name "Senlow" was derived by combing the words "senior" and "low income," the two subpopulations targeted as the primary concerns of the system.) The handi-bus operates from 8 a.m. to 5:00 p.m., and all riders must pay the same price for a one-way fare.

With 18 participants, the Kearney focus group meeting was a little larger than the Norfolk meeting, but not unusually large like the Scottsbluff/Gering meeting. The meeting was held in a centrally located church shortly after lunch. Because of the timing of the meeting, all of the participants in the focus group were senior citizens who regularly rode the handi-bus. Observations recorded in the meeting clearly reflected the perspective of the elderly. The Kearney focus group began like the other two, with participants contributing more observations on how vital the system was to the daily lives of elderly residents.

Unfortunately, this sentiment quickly gave way to fairly emotional observations about how the elderly felt forsaken by the Senlow Transportation System. One man said,

> There is only one system for too many people. The bus used to be for seniors only. Now it has become public transportation for everyone to use. The system's priorities have changed, and now service is unsatisfactory. Seniors are not getting the attention they used to get.

Another participant stated his observations on the need for more services like this: "The Senlow system needs expanding. More drivers, more buses, more money, more organization, and more adult personnel in the bus office. And, if you are meant to serve seniors, Senlow, then serve them as a priority!"

The focus group part of our research project provided added insight into the Nebraska transit study. Although the focus group sample was not representative of all of the 13 communities in the study, it did provide "meat on the bones" that converged with observations made from other investigations in the research project. In short, Nebraska handi-bus transit services play an important role in the daily lives of transit disadvantaged in medium-sized communities. Also, it appears that these transit services are stretched very thin and could easily use more resources to both meet existing demand and unmet transit needs. The stories the focus group participants told of the day-to-day impact of transit services forced NDOT to reevaluate its transit plans for these communities and look at them from a more human scale.

The impact of the study in Kearney was most dramatic. Local citizens and community leaders organized the Transportation Steering Committee to pursue increased transit options more aggressively; two new trolleys will operate on a fixed-route system. In Norfolk, a more simple need was addressed. Shortly after the focus group meeting, the transit company began providing service over the lunch hour.

INTEGRATING TECHNOLOGY WITH FOCUS GROUP RESEARCH

Technological innovations for recording focus group meetings are extremely affordable even for the smallest focus group research projects.

Digital voice recorders have replaced tape recorders as the basic equipment for recording focus group meetings. They are affordable and have operational benefits that make the research easier to conduct. They are easy to use, compact, and have a longer recording time (up to eight hours or more) without the annoying "click" of a tape running out. The data can be downloaded to a computer or other electronic storage device.

A digital voice recorder has a few specifications that a planner needs to be aware of before making a purchase. The most important is memory. The higher the memory, the more hours of the focus group meeting you can record. Memory is measured in megabytes (MB). Digital voice recorder memory capacity ranges from 16MB, which provides two hours of recording, to 62MB, which provides eight hours. Some recorders come with an expansion slot so additional memory can be added. The larger the focus group research project, the more cost-effective it becomes to purchase a digital voice recorder with a higher memory capability.

If you plan to integrate the research data with a computer, connectivity and compatibility specifications are also important. Connectivity features allow you to download audio files from a voice recorder to a computer or other electronic digital storage device. There are several benefits to downloading focus group meetings onto a computer: It frees up memory space on the voice recorder; provides a simple electronic storage format, and makes it easy to share recorded focus group meetings.

DISCUSSION QUESTIONS

1. How would focus group research for a city comprehensive plan differ from a focus group study analyzing the location of a new community recreation center?
2. Develop a multi-point focus group recruitment strategy for a research project analyzing the development of a new bicycle path through your downtown. How would different recruitment strategies (door-to-door recruiting and Facebook advertisements) attract different community groups to your meetings?
3. Interview guides are a critical component in focus group research because they allow you to compare observations made in one focus group session to the other sessions. How do you go about analyzing comments made in focus group meetings that are extremely relevant to your research topic, but fall outside of your interview guide?

REFERENCES

[1] Krueger, R., and Casey, M.A. 2000. *Focus Groups* (3rd ed.). Thousand Oaks, CA: Sage Publications, p. 26.

[2] Delbecq, A., Van de Ven, A., and Gustafson, D. 1975. *Group Techniques for Program Planning: A Guide to Nominal Group and Delphi Process*. Glenview, IL: Scott, Foresman, & Company, p. 26.

[3] Stewart, D., and Shamdasani, P. 1990. *Focus Groups: Theory and Practice*. Newbury Park, CA: Sage Publications, p. 23.

[4] Rubin, H., and Rubin, I. 1995. *Qualitative Interviewing: The Art of Hearing Data*. Thousand Oaks, CA, Sage Publications, p. 1.

[5] Rubin and Rubin, *Qualitative Interviewing*, pp. 130–131.

[6] Rubin and Rubin, *Qualitative Interviewing*, p. 130.

[7] Rubin and Rubin, *Qualitative Interviewing*, p. 131.

[8] U.S. Department of Transportation, Federal Highway Administration, and Nebraska Department of Roads, City of Lincoln. 1999. *"O" Street Improvements from 52nd Street to Wedgewood Drive, Lincoln, Nebraska*, Draft Environmental Assessment, EACNH-STPAA-34-6(124), p. 26.

[9] U.S. Department of Transportation and Nebraska Department of Roads, *"O" Street Improvements*, p. 27.

[10] Andersen, M. 1999. "East O decision on hold as council peers into future", *Lincoln Journal Star*, February 23, p. B1.

[11] Andersen, M. 1999. "O Street construction options have residents angry, confused", *Lincoln Journal Star*, February 7, p. B1.

[12] Andersen, M., "O Street construction options," p. B3.

[13] *Lincoln Journal Star*. 2000. "City Council didn't flinch on O street", January 26, p. A6.

[14] Passwell, R., and Edelstein, P. 1976. "A study of travel and behavior of the elderly," *Transportation Planning and Technology*, 3, p. 154.

5

CONTENT ANALYSIS AND
META-ANALYSIS

WHAT IS CONTENT ANALYSIS AND META-ANALYSIS?

Content analysis describes a research technique where a planner makes observations by systematically analyzing written or spoken communication, such as planning commission meeting transcripts concerning a proposed subdivision, to systematically assess who said what about the project. Content analysis is commonly associated with secondary data—data slices generated by one person or government agency that are analyzed and applied in a research project by someone else. (Primary data are generated and used by the same researcher.) Newspaper articles are one example of secondary data commonly used by planners in content analysis. Content analysis usually samples a smaller field of textual resources within a shorter time period than meta-analysis.

Meta-analysis allows you to analyze different research reports and articles in one research project. Unlike content analysis, meta-analysis uses only published secondary data, such as research reports and articles written by government agencies, universities, and nonprofit research-based or service-based organizations. You then use content analysis to analyze each publication within the meta-analysis research project.

An example would be looking at the problem of homelessness in Los Angeles and critically analyzing (using content analysis) research reports written by city, county, regional, and state governments; local universities; and local nonprofit homeless service organizations. Meta-analysis has been widely used for quantitative applications in the past; it provides a single set of numbers that describe and summarize the results of independent pieces of research. More recent applications, though, especially in the social sciences, use it for both quantitative and qualitative research.

WHY DO PLANNERS NEED CONTENT ANALYSIS AND META-ANALYSIS?

Planners commonly use content analysis to assess three types of communications: meetings, communications with the planning agency, and published reports. Meetings include any transcribed public meeting where each individual participating in the conversation is clearly identified (for example, neighborhood resident "Beth," who lives near the proposed site for a group home). Communications include written text (letters, e-mail) to the planning agency in regard to a specific situation. For example, during web-based citizen participation in Clark County, Nevada, planners analyzed e-mail messages regarding a visual preference survey of Mopa Valley. [1] The types of published reports you will analyze include newspaper articles, press releases, research reports, and planning documents. An example of a content analysis of newspaper articles would be tracking community attitudes toward group homes sited in local neighborhoods.

One reason you will pursue content analysis is to focus on the *manifest content* of the text to analyze those "elements that are physically present and countable." [2] In this quantitative approach to content analysis, you will measure text by the intensity of the number of times a word or phrase is used; examine it longitudinally to see how events, knowledge, or perceptions evolve over time; or assess the patterns in the text to see what people say. Another use for content analysis is to analyze the *latent content* of a text to provide more of a qualitative approach to interpreting the data to learn what they mean. Here, you will pay particular attention to matching issues with particular interest groups to determine who said what. Ideally, you will pursue both manifest (quantitative) and latent (qualitative) content approaches in your content analysis research to achieve a precise and an accurate account of the text. However, when facing tight deadlines and even tighter budgets, you may have to choose just one approach.

In addition to the type of data accessed through content analysis, planners also pursue this line of research for very practical reasons. Content analysis is an unobtrusive and convenient way to analyze spoken and written data. With content analysis focusing on the text of what was said, you don't have to worry about "researcher bias" influencing participant responses. Further, the convenience of analyzing published text makes this line of research extremely flexible when combined with other research strategies in a mixed method research project. As we will discuss later in this chapter, recording and archiving communicative data electronically allows you to analyze it with text-based research software.

Meta-analysis provides you with three big-picture perspectives about what is written and not written about your research topic. Meta-analysis provides a landscape of research reports and articles about the topic of interest. In the case of an analysis of homelessness in Los Angeles, meta-analysis will find reports that look at homelessness from the standpoints of issues like affordable housing, substance abuse, mental illness, deinstitutionalization, domestic violence, economic restructuring, urban sprawl, job training, and public transportation.

Meta-analysis also shows you where current research findings converge and diverge. For example, all research reports on Los Angeles's homeless agree that the lack of affordable housing is a primary contributor to the problem, but some differ on how significantly urban sprawl contributes to homelessness. Lastly, meta-analysis shows the planner where there are gaps in the current research. For example, very little research has focused on homelessness among undocumented immigrants in Los Angeles. These gaps provide a jumping-off point for future research.

These three aspects of meta-analysis are not mutually exclusive because by the end of the research project, they will provide you with an overview of what is known about the topic, where contemporary research findings converge and diverge, and show gaps in the current understanding about a topic that needs more attention in the future.

In addition to the empirical reasons, meta-analysis is a convenient research strategy for planners who want to access a tremendous amount of information to analyze as time permits. More importantly, meta-analysis is an affordable way to access research information without having to go through the time, training, and infrastructure investment to carry out original research. For planners working in cities with several research universities, state agencies, or nonprofit organizations, meta-analysis is a great way to get quality research findings without having to reinvent the wheel.

WHEN DO PLANNERS USE CONTENT ANALYSIS AND META-ANALYSIS?

You will use content analysis to figure out what transpired in a series of meetings or what was published in public reports or articles to help answer your research question. By systematically analyzing written or spoken communications, you will learn the experiences, motives, and interests of different community residents, order them in terms of intensity, and compare them to observations generated from other research projects. To do this, you must first be able to secure accurate texts of conversations, reports, or news stories that can also be archived for further analysis.

Observations generated through meta-analysis are particularly insightful when you need a big-picture understanding about a research problem. More than that, you can get a global perspective with a minimum investment of time, energy, and cost. The challenge of meta-analysis, as it is for content analysis, is to access printed research reports.

DOING CONTENT ANALYSIS AND META-ANALYSIS
Content Analysis

"There is no simple right way to do content analysis." [3] This is especially true in planning, where almost every problem faced is unique and requires adjustments in the research design to fit the particulars of the question. There is, however, a series of steps you need to follow to conduct a methodologically defendable content analysis.

Setting Up

First, identify the research variables. They provide you with the framework to organize and develop your coding scheme, which is discussed in a later section. In identifying research variables for your content analysis, keep in mind three guidelines that you must have before you begin: a good understanding of the research topic, the identity of the particular significant voices in the text, and the relationship of the different individuals and groups to the research topic. (See Table 5.1.) Identifying research variables in line with these three characteristics allows you to better understand the analyzed text by concentrating on who is talking and what they are talking about.

Second, think about the text you are about to evaluate and whether you will do manifest or latent analysis. Think about the text and which technique is better suited to it. Extensive transcripts of meetings or communications work well with both manifest and latent analysis. On the other hand, published reports and newspaper articles, especially when there are only a few, tend to work better with a latent content analysis (for example, identifying the major findings in the reports). An exception to this would be if several reports or articles over a fairly long period of time were put through a content analysis. Then, a longitudinal manifest content analysis would work well; this technique investigates several publications within a specific time frame (for example, five years) to track how subjects change over time. An example would be looking at newspaper articles containing local perceptions of neighborhood group homes and analyzing how they have changed over the last 10 years.

Table 5.1 Characteristics Associated with Content Analysis Variables

Variable Characteristic	Example
1. Research topic	Proposed projects, zoning changes, comprehensive plan
2. Individual or interest group "voices"	Individuals: Neighborhood residents, business owners, park consumers, community resident. Interest groups: Organized neighborhood residents, chamber of commerce, business associations, environmental groups
3. Relation of person (or group) to the research topic	Residents living in the project area, residents living outside of the project area
A. How do they define the topic?	"I oppose all group homes in our neighborhood because they will lower our housing values."
B. How do they differentiate it from other topics?	"I would rather have a recycling sorting facility in our neighborhood than a group home."
C. How do the person's (or group's) comments compare to other comments?	Neighborhood residents oppose the group home while city health and social service officials explain that there is a critical shortage of group homes in the community

Getting the Data

The data you will analyze come in the form of text or sound. If you are lucky, they will be available in both electronic and hard copy formats. You should carefully consider doing content analysis if the data come only in an audio format, however. Transcribing an audio database, especially a large one (more than five hours of content), may not be the best use of research resources—other alternatives may be more efficient and generate similar observations.

Getting a representative text data sample from which to conduct a content analysis is usually not a significant problem. Generally speaking, planners are more likely to use primary data (focus group meetings, e-mail comments) than secondary data and will most likely have all the text that represents an entire possible data population (for example, all the focus group transcripts), creating 100 percent coverage of the total text data population. Keep in mind that the text population may not be a representative sample of the entire community population—100 e-mail messages sent to the department's webpage represent only 1 percent of the total population in a city with a population of 10,000 residents. This is rarely a concern in content analysis sampling strategies, however, because this line of research tends to identify the available text population as the total possible population that provided comments.

Taking a sample is when the planner generates observations from a smaller subpopulation (n) which was obtained from the larger total population (N). How much you can generalize your content analysis depends on whether your strategy uses *random* or *nonrandom* sampling. Random sampling (also called probability sampling) is a technique that ensures all sampled texts have the same chance of being included in the sample of text. The random sampling process for selecting text provides you with the highest level of generalizability. If sampling is done correctly, you can be confident that your content analysis observations cover the entire sampled population of text.

Random sampling is commonly broken down into four types of strategies. (See Table 5.2.) *Simple* random sampling covers the entire population of sampled texts when each text has an equal opportunity of being selected. After enumerating the total population (N) of text, you apply a randomization device—pulling names out of a hat—to determine which texts to analyze. *Systematic random sample* is widely used by planners because of its simplicity. Systematic random sampling is when the planner selects every ith at equal intervals throughout the study population (e.g. one out of every five persons would be 3, 8, 13, etc.). In *stratified* random sampling you will segment the total population (N) into categories, then select an independent sample (n) from each stratum. Accordingly, you can speak with confidence about a specific subpopulation of text. Finally, *cluster* random sampling applies when you cannot clearly define the total population (N) of the text, but have a series of large clusters of text. In this technique, you will independently sample (n) each cluster group of texts then collectively organize them into one content analysis.

Two more common random sampling mistakes are sampling error and sampling bias. *Sampling error*, also known as sampling variability, is the amount of variation in the sampled population in comparison to the study population. A sampled population will always have some variability in relation to the study population because it is a subset of the target population and does not account for every variation in the target population. You can mitigate the amount of sampling error by: (1) increasing the size of the sampled population, and/or (2) picking a sampling strategy that allows for a closer fit of the sampled population to the target population. *Sampling bias* is created during the random sampling process where the selection process adopted by the planner produces a biased

Table 5.2 Probability Sampling Strategies

	Simple random	Systematic	Stratified	Cluster
Definition	Equal probability of selection where units are drawn from a population list	Equal probability of selection sample where a random start is chosen and every unit that falls at a certain interval from the first unit is selected	Either equal or unequal probability of selection sample where population is divided into strata (groups) and a simple random sample of each stratum is selected	Clusters that contain members of the study population are selected by a simple random sample and all members of the selected clusters are included in the study
Requirements	List of study population Count of study population (N) Sample size (n) Random selection mechanism (list of random numbers)	List of physical representation of study population Approximate count of study population (N) Sample size (n) Sampling interval ($I = N/n$) Random start	List of study population divided into strata Count for each strata Sample size for each stratum (n1, n2, etc.) Random selection used in each stratum	List of clusters All members of study population in one cluster Count of clusters (C) Approximate size of clusters (Nc) Number of sampled clusters (c) Random selection mechanism
Benefits	Easy to administer Self-weighting	Easy to administer	Reduces standard error Disproportionate stratifications can be used to increase sample size of subpopulations	List of study population is unnecessary Clusters can be stratified

sampled population (n) that only partially resembles the total population (N). For example, if you are analyzing transit demand focus group transcript data where the total focus group population is equally split (50/50) between residents who take the subway-to-work in comparison to drive-to-work and you notice that 80 percent of your sampled text is made up of drive-to-work participants, you have got sampling bias. The easiest way to protect yourself from sampling bias is to visually inspect the sampled population before you analyze the data to see if it closely resembles your total population characteristics.

Nonrandom sampling (also called *nonprobability* sampling) is usually easier to assemble, but suffers from lack of generalizability because you cannot speak with confidence about the entire text population. There are four commonly used nonrandom sampling strategies. (See Table 5.3.) In *systematic* sampling, you pick every nth text from a list. The benefit of systematic sampling is its fast process for selecting and sampling text; on the downside, the order of the text list and the pattern of text selection introduces bias into the systematic sample. *Convenience sampling* is when you choose your sample based on what you have at the time of the study. *Purposive sampling* is when you pick text out of a pool of texts based on your knowledge of the research topic and the appropriateness of the text relating to that topic. Many times you are pressed for time and may need to apply a convenience sample. *Similar/dissimilar* sampling is when you specifically target text pools that are extremely similar or dissimilar to what you are investigating. This type of sampling is commonly used in "best-practice" research where planning interventions you are looking at are either idealized or disasters you want to avoid.

Organizing the Data

No content analysis is better than its categories. [4] Once you have assembled your population of text for analysis, you must develop a series of categories so you can conduct the content analysis itself. Categories are the variables that connect the research question to the content analysis. As previously shown in Table 5.1, you should define your content analysis variables according to topic, individual (or interest group), and the relationship of person (or group) to the topic. Content analysis categories are mutually exclusive (or as close as possible) compartments under which texts are grouped.

Categories are commonly termed "codes" in the content analysis literature. Imagine that each category represents a separate file in a filing cabinet. Each word, sentence, and paragraph in the text can be placed in an individual categorical file folder with a specific heading. You will collectively organize individual categories

Table 5.3 Nonprobability Sampling Strategies

	Systematic	Convenience Sample	Purposeful Sample	Similar/Dissimilar Case
Defintion	Equal probability of selection sample where a random start is chosen and every unit that falls at a certain interval from the first unit is selected	Select cases based on their availability for the study	Select cases based on their ability to meet specific elements	Select cases that are judged to represent similar conditions or, alternatively, very different conditions
Requirements	List of physical characteristics of study population Approximate count of study population (N) Sample size (n) Sampling interval (I = N/n) Random start	Clear identification of target population Knowledge of the most convenient location of the target population	Clear identification of target population Select cases that are known beforehand that will provide useful information	Clear identification of target population Clear identification of similar/dissimilar cases Select cases that are known beforehand that will provide useful information
Benefits	Easy to administer	Saves time, money, and effort	Small samples that generate information directly related to the research question	Provides decision makers with information that is either salient to what they are experiencing, or is outside the norm of expectation in their community

on a coding sheet (also called coding scheme or coding frame), which is used to analyze the text.

Three categories exist here: words, themes, and concepts. Words, the smallest unit of analysis, are almost always used in a manifest content analysis to analyze frequency and intensity. For example, a word category can be "support." Themes usually describe a sentence (but not always) that has a string of words conveying an idea. Within the theme is at least one word connected to a person, topic, or relationship. Planners commonly use themes in manifest content analysis. The statement: "I support the proposed park in my neighborhood" shows an example of a theme.

Concepts are the largest categorical unit. A concept can be as small as a couple of sentences or as large as several paragraphs. Concepts tend to fall out of the capabilities of quantitative manifest analysis because of their size and the multiple categories of words and themes embedded in them, but provide the building blocks of most qualitative latent content analysis. An example of a concept category would be: "I do not support the proposed park. I think it will bring gangs and will be an eyesore in the neighborhood."

There are a few ways to create a coding sheet. One way is to create it strictly according to the research variables identified at the start of the content analysis without looking at the text. This is called *deductive coding*. This process ensures that the identified categories are closely tethered to the research question. Or you can take an opposite approach and create a coding sheet by reading the text first and developing the categories from what you read. This strategy is called *inductive coding* and it allows you to firmly ground your categories in the text. You usually apply this type of data-up coding when you have limited knowledge about what is going on in the text. A third approach is called *summative coding* and does both deductive and inductive coding in one study. In this strategy, you will first identify several categories that directly relate to the research question before looking at the text. As you read the text, you will add new categories discovered from the material and eliminate those categories not pertinent to the text. We suggest you opt for the third approach because it combines the benefits of generating text-specific categories (also called grounded categories) through the open-coding reading of the text, with the quality check of having predefined codes that are closely connected to the research question.

The analysis of *New York Times* articles addressing the issue of "homelessness" by Takashi and Gaber provides an illustration. [5] In the early 1990s, they were researching popular perceptions of homelessness in New York City. One of our questions involved the local government's concerns regarding municipal shelter siting. To get data on this topic they did a purposeful sample of *New York Times* articles between 1980 and 1990 that discussed the siting of city homeless shelters

Table 5.4 Final Category System of Local Government Concerns from *New York Times* Review

# of Units (N=53)	What are the Local Government Concerns Regarding Analysis of Municipal Shelter Siting?
n=15	I. Communities do not accept shelters/shelters disrupt communities – community opposition high – shelters politically difficult
n=9	II. Lack of planning foresight coordination – no other plans – no long-range plans
n=7	III. City not giving enough help to homeless – supply of shelter beds does not meet demand – city should do more
n=7	IV. Cost – small shelters too costly
n=6	V. In-fighting amongst local state actors – city count president criticizes mayor – Brooklyn borough president criticizes board of estimate
n=5	VI. Size of shelters – large shelters opposed – small shelters too costly
n=4	VII. Need to use available buildings – schools preferable to armories – need buildings with toilets and showers

in New York. A total of 53 articles were identified that specifically addressed this issue. Table 5.4 shows the results of the manifest content analysis. As it reveals, the most frequently mentioned concern in the *New York Times* is that "communities do not accept shelters/shelters disrupt communities" (n=15). This was followed by "lack of planning/foresight" (n=9), "city not giving enough to help the homeless" (n=7), and "costs" (n=7).

Analyzing the Data

Although each content analysis is case-specific and no two analyses are completely alike, there are four general types of investigations. (See Table 5.5.) An *intensity investigation* looks at the significance of a word/concept in the text. In this case, you can use a manifest approach and do a word frequency/category count, or take a latent approach and look at the power of words in a "key-word-in-context" (kwic) [6] list to see how the word is used in a sentence or for contextual meaning.

Table 5.5 Common Types of Content Analysis Investigation Used by Planners

Type of Investigation	Type of Content Analysis	Type of Coding
Intensity	Manifest	a. word frequency b. category count
	Latent	a. key-word-in-context b. open reading
Trend	Manifest	a. word frequency b. category count
	Latent	a. open reading
Identification/Definition	Latent	a. key-word-in-context b. open reading
Patterns	Manifest	a. word frequency b. category count
	Latent	a. key-word-in-context b. open reading

A *trend analysis* looks at the longitudinal evolution of the text data over time. You can select a manifest approach and do a word frequency count to see how the intensity of specific words changes over time, or do a category count and evaluate the rise and fall of different categories over time. A latent trend analysis requires you to carefully read the text over time and document how the community's thinking about a particular topic evolved. An *identification/definition investigation* is largely a latent content analysis where you will closely examine how topics are defined. For example, is the proposed neighborhood park identified as an opportunity or a threat? Finally, a *pattern investigation* involves going through the text to look at the consistent connections between topics and individuals, such as whether neighborhood residents support a proposed park. In a *manifest analysis*, you perform a word frequency count/category count, while in a latent analysis you can choose a "kwic" to see how different groups view a topic, or pursue an open read of the text to evaluate the larger context of a topic.

Meta-Analysis

Getting quality text data is crucial in meta-analysis.[i] Like all secondary data research strategies, meta-analysis is only as good as the available data. Consequently meta-analysis suffers from the GIGO syndrome: Garbage In, Garbage Out. No matter how well you conduct a meta-analysis, if the text data are suspect, the research findings are also suspect. Below, we discuss the linear steps to help you execute a successful meta-analysis.

Setting Up

There are four basic parts to a meta-analysis: (1) variable specificity, (2) publication type, (3) acceptable publication sources, and (4) publishing time frame. Controlling these allows you to execute an efficient and focused investigation without becoming overwhelmed by an infinite amount of text data or underwhelmed with only a trickle of text to analyze.

Begin your meta-analysis investigation by specifying the research variables in the project. These variables become the points of query when you search for secondary data text. This process is like a fisherman standing on the shore casting his net out to the ocean to catch fish. The less specific the variables, the wider the net is cast (and the more publications you will review in your investigation). For example, you may be interested in developing an affordable housing plan for recently resettled refugees in a city. You decide upon a meta-analysis to learn the major understandings, issues, and applications of this topic. If you query generic variables like "affordable housing" or "refugees," you will most likely be overwhelmed by too many publications to review, few of which may relate to the original research question. However, if you more narrowly define your research variables to focus the query on "refugee housing," you will find fewer documents to review, and the majority, if not all, will be focused solely on your research interest. Like the seasoned fisherman casting his net to the ocean, the skilled planning researcher learns from practice to accurately define research variables in the casting stage of meta-analysis.

In the next step, determine what publications are in your net and identify their sources. Unlike content analysis, which mostly focuses on one type of text from one source (for example, focus group transcripts or newspaper articles), meta-analysis investigations cover a wider range of texts. This fact is both a strength and potential weakness. You must first establish what type of publication you are interested in analyzing. If you want a bigger snapshot of the data, review a wider range of publications to increase the chances that your analysis will cover a larger context from a diverse range of perspectives, such as journal and newspaper articles, published research reports, and government documents. The risk you take by increasing the diversity of publications involves the potential problem of analyzing texts that are not easily comparable. For example, it would be hard to compare a one-page *New York Times* article on resettling refugees to a comprehensive 200-page report on the same topic conducted by the Federal Office of Refugee Resettlement.

Once the type of text data is established, focus your attention on where to get them. List all the organizations (public, private, nonprofit, educational, newspapers) that potentially published something related to the identified research variables. There are two competing strategies for listing potential data sources. In one you "open up" the list to cover as many potential data sources as possible with the intent of increasing the diversity of perspectives represented in the research topic. The risk here is that too comprehensive a list increases the likelihood of getting publications from questionable sources. This is the GIGO syndrome raising its ugly head again. The strategy to choose to address potential questions of internal validity is to limit your list of sources to known organizations having a reputation for producing solid research.

The research variables themselves usually determine the time frame of the publications to be reviewed in the meta-analysis. For example, for the meta-analysis on housing services for resettling refugees, you may be interested in looking at recent practices in the last 10 years. The conventional wisdom regarding the publication time frame is that the longer the time frame, the less the chance of missing a well-worn practice or knowledge base used in the past. On the other hand, increasing the time frame for reviewable publications may force you to wade through an unnecessary amount of texts having little or no relevance to the contemporary problems you are researching.

Setting up the meta-analysis according to the four points mentioned above will help you control the number of publications to be reviewed and make the study more manageable. (See Table 5.6.) If you are initially overwhelmed with too many publications to review, reframe the variables to be more specific, narrow the pool of acceptable types of publications, limit the publications sources to only a few specific organizations, or shorten the time frame for qualifying text. If you feel you are not reviewing enough publications, you can open the breadth of the research variables, expand the type of publications reviewed, look to a wider range of publication sources, or increase the time frame for acceptable publications.

Getting the Data

Getting data for meta-analysis involves searching for publications that relate to your identified research variables. You need to make the process of obtaining your publications as comprehensive and transparent as possible to prevent any suspicions of sampling bias and to show you have exhausted every possible avenue to find research-related publications. To do this, keep a record of where you looked for data. Invariably, you will miss one key publication in the data-gathering process. But with a good accounting system of where you looked for data, you can retrace your steps and go back and get it.

Table 5.6 Four Adjustable Parts of Meta-Analysis

Narrower Focus	Adjustable Part	Expanding Focus
Define the research variables more narrowly by allowing only publications that directly relate to the research variables	Variable specificity	Define the variables more broadly to incorporate more contextually related publications to the research variables
Narrow the pool of qualifying publications to a small number of sources (for example, only research reports)	Publication type	Open the criteria for allowing a wide range of publications (for example, journal articles, research reports)
Rely only on established publication sources (for example, peer review research journals, government reports)	Publication source	Be less discriminating when determining allowable publication sources
Define a narrow time frame to prevent older and potentially outdated publications from being analyzed in the investigation	Publication time frame	Define a large time allowing for older publications to be included in the study to prevent reinventing of the wheel

Searches for publications usually take one or a combination of two forms. The easiest way is to comb through publication indices of research journals, government documents, and newspaper articles, looking for publications related to research variables. For example, LexisNexis and Google Scholar are very popular searchable, online full-text archives that cover research articles, government reports, legislative materials, and court decisions. [7]

The other search method is through old-fashioned "cold calls," where you contact organizations directly to see if they have any publications related to your research variables. In the age of the Internet, this cold-calling has become less popular, though it is still important, particularly in small towns or rural areas where all reports may not be on the Internet. Most likely, you will use both processes to look for the publications you need. As we will see later, your records of the organizations you contact will be very valuable to the study even if the organization does not have any publications to contribute to the investigation. The list establishes your exhaustive and complete "cast" for documents.

Organizing the Data

Your data organization should take shape in an ongoing process during the data-gathering stage. This way all the texts are already loosely organized when you start to review them critically in the data analysis stage.

Your data organization begins with a topical division of texts into distinct categories. For example, in doing a meta-analysis on housing for recently resettled refugees, you can divide the texts into two categories: refugee demographics and refugee housing. As in content analysis, you can choose to develop the organizing categories either by the predefined research variable, or from what you gleaned from the documents, or a combination of the two. Within each category, you should divide the data further by type of publication (for example, government reports and newspaper articles). This is especially relevant if you have a particularly open text search and will review several different types of documents.

Analyzing the Data

Analyzing the data in a meta-analysis involves a careful reading of each publication and searching out relevant concepts as they relate to the research variables. Given the magnitude and diversity of texts reviewed in a meta-analysis, you may need to take a latent content analysis approach to analyzing the publications. As in the identification/definition type of content analysis investigation, you will look for texts that identify key issues and define their significance. At the end of your analysis, you will produce a detailed summary of each document (including author and publication date), connecting findings in the texts to the research variables developed in the set-up stage of the investigation.

The explanatory power of meta-analysis takes shape when you organize the summaries into a meta-analysis matrix. This allows you to compare and contrast all of the analyzed documents according to the established set of variables. The matrix is organized with the identification of each reviewed text on the far left-hand column, each addressing the same research variables listed in the top horizontal column. (See Table 5.7.) You then insert a precise account per variable from each publication. For example, in the case of the analysis on housing for resettled refugees, you would plug in each publication account as it relates to the variables, number of refugees, type of housing, and funding for housing. You must remember that *not* recording an observation on a particular variable is just as important as recording an avalanche of observations per variable.

Table 5.7 Anatomy of the Meta-Analysis Matrix (Refugee Housing)

Publications	Research Variables		
	Variable A (Number of Refugees)	Variable B (Type of Refugee Housing)	Variable C (Funding for Refugee Housing)
Government Reports			
1.			
2.			
3.			
Journal Research Articles			
1.			
2.			
3.			
Newspaper Articles			
1.			
2.			
3.			

Statistical techniques used in meta-analysis strive to standardize the observations from the multiple sources of data and translate them into one statistical measurement. You can use a combination of two established meta-analysis techniques, "narrative procedure" and "vote counting," to allow for a collective analysis of the disparate text. The narrative procedure requires you to read each document, then construct an overarching written picture of the accounts presented in the publication. Vote counting is basically tabulating the distribution of different assessments among the reviewed publications and identifying the most common shared observations. [8] The written accounts of each text are entered into the meta-analysis matrix.

Table 5.7 illustrates a framework for a meta-analysis about refugee housing. The matrix compares and contrasts the various publications reviewed in the analysis as they relate to the research variables. By analyzing the various observations among the publications, the planner determined areas of concentration in the sampled publications (demographics and funded housing) and identified low points (type of housing).

QUESTIONS OF INTERNAL AND EXTERNAL VALIDITY AND ISSUES OF RELIABILITY IN CONTENT ANALYSIS AND META-ANALYSIS

Unlike field research, focus groups, and photographic investigations, content analysis and meta-analysis do not generate primary data. These research strategies focus on the sampling process to obtain primary or secondary data and then analyze the text data. As a result, questions of internal and external validity in text-based research focus on how you obtain (sample) the data and your system for analyzing it. You will have an easier time dealing with questions of validity and reliability when you work with primary data you generated, because you have first-hand knowledge of how the data were obtained (for example, focus group). When the research moves to secondary text data—with multiple types of documents from several authors—managing questions of validity and reliability becomes more complicated.

Questions of Internal Validity

Questions of internal validity in content analysis and meta-analysis focus on the planner's conclusions. In this case, the majority of empirical questions associated with internal validity orbit around three topics: sampling validity, comparability, and semantic validity. (See Table 5.8.) "Face validity" is a fourth type, mostly discussed in cases of content analysis. There will be more on these questions later in this chapter.

The overarching question in *internal sampling validity* asks if the sample text accurately represents the text population. Since questions of sampling validity in content analysis of primary data rest on the method that generates the text in the first place (for example, focus groups, field interviews), it is not necessary to discuss questions of this type for text data because the analyzed text represents 100 percent of the sample.

When you question internal validity and secondary data, however, it is different. Questions about sampling validity with secondary data ask: (1) To what extent does a "sample accurately represent the population from which it is drawn?" and (2) To what extent does a "sample accurately represent a population or phenomenon other than that from which it is drawn?" [9] The first question focuses on the sampling strategy you used to obtain the analyzed text. Here, the reader evaluating the internal validity of a content analysis or meta-analysis investigation looks to see if you chose the most appropriate sampling strategy per sampled text population (for example, random versus nonrandom sampling)

Table 5.8 Most Common Questions of Internal Validity in Content Analysis and Meta-Analysis

Type of Question	Content Analysis		Meta-Analysis
	Primary Data	Secondary Data	Secondary Data
I. Sampling A. Not a representative sample	Not applicable	Did not sample enough text within a source	Did not get a representative sample from all recognized sources
B. Not sampling the right text	Not applicable	Missed the right literature	Unbalanced sample from different sources
II. Comparability A. Incomparable text	Not applicable	Not likely to be a problem if kept to one text	Comparing texts that should not be compared
III. Semantic A. Variable not matching textual meaning	Less likely a problem if variables are connected to text	Difficult to match terms from multiple authors	Significant question when looking at different types of documents by different authors
B. Exclusivity of variables	Less likely a problem if variables are connected to text	More likely a problem as more documents by different authors are analyzed	Impossible to be achieved. Can best be approximated by grounding variables to text
IV. Face Validity A. Findings do not match or resemble other established research findings	Does it make sense?	Does it make sense?	Does it make sense?

and if you reviewed enough text to make sure it is representative of the entire sampled text population.

The second question looks at how representative the text is of the research topic. One of the most common problems of sampling validity occurs when the planner discovers a well-documented research topic, but it does not discuss the specific area or angle needed for the project. For example, a Birmingham, Alabama, planner doing a meta-analysis on resettling refugees will find a wealth of texts dealing with this research topic at a national level, as well as several case studies throughout the U.S., but very few resources, if any, that focus solely on resettling refugees in the Birmingham area. Because of the gap between what is published in the text and what the planner is looking for, most content analysis and meta-analysis researchers stress that content analysis is "ineffective for testing causal relationships between variables." [10] Therefore, exercise caution before assuming that the reviewed text accurately represents the area you are investigating. You will be vulnerable to questions of representative internal validity if you draw too-specific conclusions from a text that does not closely focus on the particular location of your investigation.

Another challenge to internal validity arises when you draw conclusions from texts that have very little in common with each other, such as extensive government research reports and newspaper articles. You can take two paths to protect yourself from this problem. One is to discard publications that are spurious or clearly do not belong with the majority of the remaining text. By "cleaning up the data," you significantly eliminate the threat of incompatibility, one question of internal validity. However, this clean-up comes at the cost of discarding underrepresented perspectives that are relevant, but not up to the standard of more rigorous research reports and refereed journal articles. Eliminating some documents from the pool of reviewed texts because they are dissimilar to the other texts is problematic in itself, because you run the risk of biasing the sampled text by eliminating outlying observations.

I recommend a second path: Keep all the texts in the pool, but clearly identify the methods, data, findings, and methodological weaknesses associated with each specimen. This way, if extremely disparate texts share similar observations with the accepted mainstream publications, your confidence increases because you know that the convergence of data is fairly significant. If the same text data do not conform to the observations made by the majority of the other texts, look at the methodological profile of each renegade text to see if the difference in observations is the result of research design or the quality of the research. At the end of the content analysis, you can report a range of findings in the investigation and provide a brief explanation about why that range occurs based on the content of the reviewed text.

The question of *semantic internal validity* looks at how closely you compare the meaning of words used as your research variables to how people actually use them in the real world. This question of validity asks two interdependent questions. The first looks at how big a difference exists between the planner's definition of terms versus the authors' definition of the same words. Here, investigators look at the specific definitions of coded variables used in the content analysis set against the way the publication authors apply the same words. The validity of your content analysis rests on your ability to create categories that are mutually exclusive to the text you review.

The second question asks how exclusive the coded categories used in the content analysis are. The exclusivity of categories is defined as only one unit (word, sentence, paragraph) belonging to a specific category. You need to be extremely careful in developing your coding sheet to avoid any ambiguity about which category a unit belongs to. For some research projects, this may be more difficult than it sounds. For example, "community power" can mean either electricity or grassroots organizing and doing a content analysis about a neighborhood organizing around affordable electricity can make the coding sheet a little confusing. Crafting mutually exclusive categories on a coding sheet may be ultimately impossible, but to conduct a defendable content analysis you should strive for that goal. The easiest and most dependable way to protect yourself from questions like this is to ground as many coded variables in the text as possible. Again, grounding content analysis variables involves prereading the text to identify relevant variables to be used in the coding sheet.

Face validity is a deceptively simple assessment of internal validity. It is the acceptance of conclusions drawn from the text because on the "face of things" they appear to be obvious and make sense. There is no specific method to test for face validity. You must simply take a step back from the content analysis and, as objectively as possible, evaluate the study to see if it conforms to common sense. Face validity is growing in popularity among planners because it provides a new way to gain insight on the applicability of their research findings from a community's perspective. [11]

Questions of External Validity

Questions of external validity look at the generalizability of the planner's research findings to other case studies or to a larger theoretical discussion. In content analysis and meta-analysis, questions of external validity focus on how far the planner moves away from the representativeness of her sample to explain other situations. You can run into trouble in two ways with questions of external validity in text-based research. The first, most common way is when you make observations based on a research site that is not geographically related to the location of the site you are studying; for example, a Lincoln, Nebraska, housing planner explaining the housing needs for newly resettled refugees based on studies done in New York City.

Second, you can fail the test of external validity by improperly generalizing your observations about a topic that is closely aligned with the research but still a very different situation. An example of this failure is a housing planner applying results from a meta-analysis about housing refugees in Lincoln, Nebraska, to explaining affordable housing for homeless families. Outside of the shared problem of vulnerable families looking for a home, the circumstances surrounding the two different populations are literally worlds apart. The easiest way to protect yourself from questions of external validity is to keep your observations within the parameters of the sampled text.

Reliability

Reliability focuses on the ability of content analysis and meta-analysis to produce the same results after several trials. Three recognized threats to reliability in this line of research are stability, reproducibility, and accuracy. [12] Stability describes the degree to which observations generated from your analysis of the text do not change over time. This certainty is achieved when you come up with the same conclusions after coding the same text on repeated trials. A lack of stability occurs when you come up with different conclusions after each reading of the text.

Reproducibility is the amount of variance found when a different investigator codes the same text with the same code sheet as the original researcher. Also called inter-coder reliability, failure of this test occurs when different investigators come up with different conclusions after reading the same text.

Accuracy is the extent to which the content analysis of the text meets standard expectations of the study. This is the strongest test of reliability because it is the most difficult standard to meet. To truly establish accuracy in a content analysis and meta-analysis, compare observations from another proven study widely accepted as correct to the conclusions drawn from the original content analysis. [13]

CASE STUDY #1: CONTENT ANALYSIS OF THE WILDERNESS PARK PROJECT

Seldom discussed in the content analysis literature is how easily and conveniently the research technique can be used to get a quick read of a series of publications. This is particularly true with manifest "vote counting" content analysis research. By keeping the number of research variables used to analyze the documents very small (for example, community residents "support," "don't support," or "other" a particular planning proposal), you get a fast, systematic understanding of issues in a fairly short time.

This case study exemplifies how a planner can use transcripts from city council meetings to analyze what members of the community said in a city council hearing about a proposed zoning change. In almost all medium-sized and larger cities, it is common practice that planning commission and city council meetings are recorded and transcribed. They provide a wonderful source of spoken data because each speaker is identified by name and place of residence or organization represented. The transcribed minutes are made available to the public shortly after the meeting, in about a week or so. The transcribed minutes provide a great *ex post facto* (after-the-fact) assessment of who said what in the meeting.

Planning commission and city council meeting comments can be fairly confusing when community residents are emotional about a proposed planning action, as was the case with the Wilderness Park Project in Lincoln, Nebraska. A proposed development, which required a zoning change next to Wilderness Park, created a huge public outcry that was closely covered by the local media. Unfortunately, what the city planners heard in the meeting was "opposition," which was very different from what the community was saying: "Support the project but delay the vote." In this case study, we show how a content analysis of city council transcripts could have been used to help planners get a better understanding of what the community was saying in a relatively short period of time.

Wilderness Park is located in the southwest corner of Lincoln. Up until the early 1990s, the area around the park was mostly agricultural. Lincoln has been steadily growing to the south for the last 20 years, placing Wilderness Park on a collision course with suburban growth. The park first opened in 1972 for the purpose of flood control. The park was designed to catch floodwaters from Salt Creek, which acts as a meandering spine that runs throughout the park. Wilderness Park is a long and narrow park, stretching seven miles long, but never expanding wider than half a mile and made up of a little over 1,450 densely forested acres.

A major part of the controversy surrounding the proposed development resulted because the city had no current data on Wilderness Park. The most recent environmental assessment the planning department had of the park was done in 1971. This study was the original assessment of the Salt Creek channel, used to propose the surrounding area be converted to the park. Changes in the zoned land use in the city's 1994 comprehensive plan, which changed the area abutting Wilderness Park from agriculture to urban residential, set the stage for the debate surrounding the park.

Knowing the southeastern section of town was ripe for development, the planning department commissioned a Wilderness Park subarea plan to get a better sense of how future development may impact the park and the immediate floodplain. Before the subarea study could be completed, two real estate companies sought to develop South 14th Street and Pine Lake Road through a series of amendments with the planning commission and city council that first had the area rezoned from agriculture to I-1 zoning ("Industrial Employment"), then had the newly zoned land rezoned to a higher I-3. (See Figure 5.1.) The zoning amendments were okayed by the planning department because they conformed with the intent of the revised comprehensive plan and were quickly passed by the planning commission—until the community realized what was happening and started to ask questions in the city council meetings.

The planning department was presented with a unique window of opportunity regarding the Wilderness Park proposal.[ii] When the developers presented the project to the city council for a vote, the community comments were so intense that the council decided to delay the vote for one month so it could get more information about the proposal. During this delay, the planning department had a chance to learn more about the community interests in the project, and to see if it could broker a compromise between the local residents and the developers. The fastest and easiest way for the planning department to learn about the residents' major concerns would be to do a content analysis of the city council minutes.

Unfortunately, the city council meeting minutes were not analyzed. If they had been, the planning department would have learned that the community was not against the proposed project; they only wanted the city council vote to be delayed so the results of the subarea plan could make the proposed project more environmentally sensitive. Starting with a simple "vote counting" manifest content analysis of the city council meeting transcripts after the fact, we found the majority of the 15 people who testified in the meeting (11 out of 15) generally

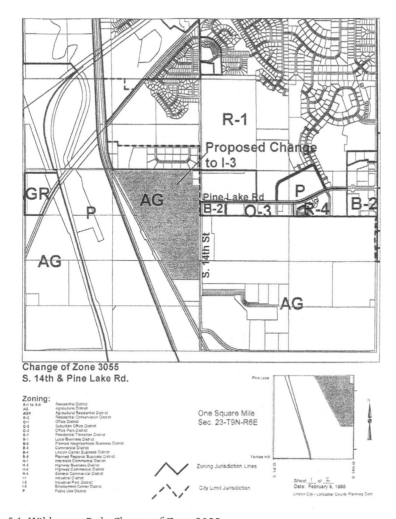

Figure 5.1 Wilderness Park: Change of Zone 3055

supported the project, with eight of these individuals wanting to delay the city council vote so the findings of the completed subarea plan could be incorporated into the proposed project. Only three of the 11 individuals completely supported the project (two of the three individuals were the developer and a representative of the local chamber of commerce). Less than one-third (four individuals) opposed the project outright.

Following up the manifest analysis with a latent content analysis of the city council transcripts showed that, among eight individuals who asked for a delay in the vote, all showed a surprising amount of support for development in the city as well as development in the Wilderness Park area. Below are a few excerpts of how residents articulated their perspectives:

> ... being a lifetime Lincoln resident, I'm not against development. My folks were born here. I was born here. ... I am not asking for development in that area to stop ... the only thing that I'd ask is to put it in pending so we at least have a chance to look at the facts [in the subarea plan] once again before we make an unwise decision like in the past.

> I am all for progress but I think it needs to be done in a very factual way, looking to the future, and not just going for it in the sake of developers. I'd like you to wait until the study's completed.

These last comments were very telling of what happened in the next city council meeting.

> I don't like coming down here because I'm not a good speaker. I talk too long. But you're going to lose a lot of support from the people. If you ask for a vote of the people and they were very well indoctrinated, this thing would be turned down so hard it would absolutely amaze you. ... There are a lot of people here that displayed a lot of courage today. I think they let it all hang out. I'm proud of them.

The planning department did not take the initiative to follow up with the community on the delayed city council vote. What happened in the following council meeting was no surprise. A large contingent of concerned citizens shared their concerns about the proposed Wilderness Park project. But as observed in the content analysis of the second city council meeting, the transcripts show that community residents had a dramatic change of heart.

Like the content analysis of the first city council meeting, a manifest "vote counting" content analysis was used to analyze the transcripts from the second meeting. As at the first meeting, 15 individuals presented their observations in the hearing. Eight of the presenters in the second meeting also spoke in the first meeting. This time, 80 percent of the individuals (12 out of 15) rejected the project outright. Only one person held out for delaying the city council vote until the subarea plan was completed; two (one of them was the developer) wholeheartedly supported the project. The sentiments of opposition are summed up by one person's testimony, obtained through a latent analysis of the meeting transcripts:

So, once this decision is made to grant this zoning, it's going to stay. And last meeting, again somebody recited a nursery rhyme or story and that kind of makes me think of one, too, about the camel and his master crossing the desert. They pitched a tent at night and the camel said it's cold, can I come inside the tent and the master said no, not enough room for both of us in here. He said well, how about (I) just put my nose in the tent. And the guy said O.K. And, of course, if you know the story, first goes the nose, then the head, then his hump and the next thing you know, the whole camel's in the tent and the master's out in the cold. I think at this point, if you approve this project without the Wilderness Park study, it's going to be the public left out in the cold.

The city council voted unanimously to support the proposed project along Wilderness Park. Although the outcome of this case study does not end on a positive note, it does provide a practical example of how planners can use content analysis of a published document to get a quick and non-invasive insight into what people said. Obviously, this analysis is not representative of all of the city's residents and how they feel about the Wilderness Park project. It does, however, provide the planner with a small vista on a particular situation, which can then be checked with other data sources.

CASE STUDY #2: META-ANALYSIS OF NEBRASKA SOCIAL SERVICE NEEDS

Community health and social service providers rarely have enough resources to meet all of their clients' needs. Fiscally, they operate on a patchwork of various federal, state, county, and local funding sources that come attached with requirements for the human service planner to conduct some form of research (also called "needs assessment" among social service providers) to qualify for the funds. Many times, the human services planner lacks the staff and resources to carry out the required needs assessment to qualify for the funds.

I was approached by the Nebraska Department of Social Services (NDSS) to help it conduct a state-wide human services needs assessment for the state's nine Community Action Programs (CAPs). CAPs are required by federal and state law to provide needs assessments to receive Community Service Block Grant (CSBG) funds. NDSS told us that conducting a state-wide needs assessment through a primary research strategy would be too expensive and time consuming; Nebraska is a geographically diverse state with over 77,000 square miles and two time zones. The state had dozens of state-wide and regional needs assessments and officials wanted us to analyze the reports in relation to the state and the nine regional CAP service areas. They gave us four months to complete the research.

In less than four months, I had to execute a meta-analysis of all of the needs assessments conducted in the state of Nebraska in the past 10 years. Operationally this task required us to hire research assistants, obtain all relevant human service needs assessments conducted in the state in the last 10 years, compile and analyze the data, and prepare the final report. To complement the meta-analysis, I did a longitudinal census analysis of each of the nine CAP regions to help each of their directors better understand the demographic trends of their local communities.

Fortunately, the NDSS had a very clear research objective and defined the four set-up elements for our meta-analysis for us. Variables were very open to all human service needs. I determined coding variables for the content analysis through a prereading of the assessments, grounding them from the text data.

The publications were limited to previously conducted needs assessments in the state; acceptable publications were limited to NDSS-recognized research reports by NDSS-recognized organizations. Since NDSS was interested only in recent changes in human service needs, the publishing time frame was limited to all needs assessments conducted in the last 10 years.

Getting the data presented the most problematic part of the meta-analysis investigation. None of the conducted needs assessments were listed in any indices or searchable through an Internet search engine. NDSS had only a list of state and local organizations that had needs assessments conducted for them. This information required me to do a purposeful "snowball sampling" technique to develop a list of Nebraska contacts. First, I contacted the nine community action agencies and asked for recent needs assessments. I asked each agency about other assessments that had been conducted in its region and made contact with the other agencies involved. NDSS also provided a list of agencies that had received NDSS funds to conduct an assessment.

I experienced three problems in collecting the needs assessments. The first was finding someone who knew if the organization had conducted a needs assessment, and if so, where and how it could be obtained. Finding the right person in a large organization took several calls, a countless number of intra-agency referrals, and lots of voice mail messages.

Second, I had difficulty getting copies of the organizations' reports quickly and had to politely remind some agencies how urgent their reports were for the research project. Delays in receiving reports delayed our complete content analysis of all the needs assessments. Finally, some nonprofit agencies seemed to push the operational definition of "nonprofit" by requesting high prices for their small research reports. Since we did not have a budget to purchase needs assessments, these were not included in the final analysis.

In the end, I obtained 74 needs assessment reports from the 107 agencies contacted throughout the state. As I collected the reports, I organized them into the nine regional CAP districts and then catalogued them by substantive topic (for example, elderly health care); publication source; date; methods used; type of data; findings; and recommendations. We analyzed all gathered needs assessments using a content analysis. However, the few needs assessments that appeared suspicious— for example, a focus group research investigation that had only three people in attendance, including the moderator—remained in the final study but its conclusions were footnoted as "based on a methodologically weak needs assessment."

I then organized the final report into three sections: state-wide needs assessment analysis, nine regional community action agency analyses, and the contact sheet of the 107 different organizations contacted in the meta-analysis. The state-wide investigation evaluated 14 documents that reflected the needs of the state.

The needs assessments were subdivided into eight substantive topics based on our prereading of the reports: aging; families/children/youth; health; housing/homelessness; head injuries; mental health; substance abuse; and transit. I then conducted an identification/latent content analysis of the needs assessment within each subtopic to identify some of the more prominent human service needs facing the state.

The section analyzing the community action agency needs assessments was subdivided into nine sections representing the nine CAP service areas. As I did with the state needs assessments, I subdivided the content analysis of the regional needs assessments into substantive topics based on a prereading of the documents, then conducted a combined manifest/latent content analysis of the regional needs assessments.

I began the content analysis of the documents with a manifest/intensity investigation to develop a ranking of the more common topics. This step was followed with a latent content analysis of the needs assessments to provide a context for the more intensely discussed topics. One example of how this process worked at the regional level was illustrated in the meta-analysis of needs assessments conducted in the Panhandle Community Services (PCS) service area, located in the southwestern part of Nebraska. For the PCS service area, there was clear convergence of the identified needs for better serving the aging population: out of 10 needs assessments we reviewed, four of them highlighted the need for more services for the aging population. The remaining six were scattered into several directions and did not coalesce on a shared theme.

A closer examination of the four needs assessments on aging revealed social and health issues were the most significant issues among the elderly. The need to better serve the aging population in this region of the state was further supported by the census analysis, which documented that the population aged 65 and older had increased more than 37 percent between 1970 and 1990.

The meta-analysis achieved its research objective: Identify human service needs for both the state and the nine CAP regions based on recently completed needs assessments. As required by NDSS, the investigation was completed in a short period of time. Although the meta-analysis of the needs assessments did not tell the state and regional human service providers anything remarkably new about their clients, the analysis did provide them with a more comprehensive understanding of all the recent research published on the needs in their areas and how these needs related to each other. Armed with the big-picture understanding of existing needs assessments, CAP directors are now better able to fine-tune their human service programs to match the identified needs, as well as be more informed about the direction for future needs assessments.

INTEGRATING TECHNOLOGY WITH CONTENT ANALYSIS AND META-ANALYSIS

Big Data Analytics

Big data is the collection of secondary data sets digitally stored on multiple servers. The growing interest in big data research in the last decade is in part the result of exponential growth in the amount of digital information, and government agencies providing more of their data sets to the public through website portals (e.g. data.gov). What makes big data research "big" is the amount of data that is digitally accessible to the planner. In 2000, "only one-quarter of all of the world's stored information was digital. ... Today, less than two-percent of all stored information is non-digital." [14] The evolution of government toward the greater integration of *information and communication technologies* (ICTs) in their day-to-day operations ("e-government") had a significant impact in motivating planners to conducting more secondary data research projects. [15]

Big data investigations operate differently from other types of more traditional social science research projects. In big data investigations, the planner approaches data with the intent to discover ("query") what is inside of the data. A planner conducting a big data investigation is basically an investigator exploring ("querying") databases via a series of techniques (called "data mining") that allow her to discover and analyze (previously unseen) patterns in the data. [16]

Each query the planner makes to the data warehouse pulls out a specific subset ("sample") of data.

Databases used for big data investigations are digitally stored information that hold quantitative, text, image, and geographic data on computer servers that have cleaned and organized the stored data sets. There are two types of Big Data databases. *Data warehouses* contain a very large breadth of database information and are organized according to more general themes that are accessible to everyone. An example of a data warehouse is the U.S. Federal Government data portal (data.gov) that has a relational database that contains over 194,000 databases on agriculture, climate, education, energy, finance, health, etc. *Data marts* are smaller versions (contain smaller and fewer databases) of data warehouses and are organized around a single topic (or department focus) that organizes its information according to topics relevant to the host department's interest. An example of a data mart would be a state's database on road data. Both data warehouses and data marts have "relational databases" which consist of interrelated databases that are organized by a database management software (DBMS) that allows the planner to query multiple databases at one time.

Qualitative big data analytics focuses on either words or images. Two of the more common types of text data planners access are either forums or blogs. Forum text data analysis is when you access an online forum where people post and respond to each other along a specific theme, such as subway commuting in Chicago. Blog analysis is more individualized: It requires you to analyze detailed online text on a particular topic by a set of individuals. Bloggers usually mix text and images about personal lived experiences, such as walking in New York City.

Image big data analytics is easy to access and extremely cost effective (free!). Urban landscapes, traffic corridors, and transit hubs around the world are monitored 24 hours a day, seven days week, by municipal (and some private) urban cameras (e.g. EarthCam). You literally can conduct photographic field research of an urban space from your desk. Many cities archive their urban images, allowing you to analyze urban spaces over time and in different conditions (e.g. rain) or situations (e.g. morning rush hour traffic).

There are three data mining techniques that are particularly relevant to qualitative planning research. Data mining for the purpose of *association rules* is when the planner queries the data warehouse and asks "if/then" questions when she is looking at events or characteristics that frequently occur together that are not apparent in various databases. For example, in researching African American young adults for obesity, Robinson et al. looked at a data set of 7,747 black and white youths from the National Longitudinal Study of Adolescent Health database and queried it on the relationship of: if African American, between 11 and 19, and obese, "then" in relation to socioeconomic status and gender. The researchers discovered that parental education had a significant impact in predicting gender obesity disparity in African American youths. [17]

Clustering is defined as the process of classifying a large group of data items into smaller groups that share the same or similar properties. Each cluster the planner identifies is a unit of classification that was not previously recognized in the database. In a cluster analysis, the planner is looking for two things: grouping of data points that share similar characteristics and data points that are not clustered with the shared characteristic data are called outliers. Classification operates on the same principle as clustering analysis but differs in that the planner is conducting a classification analysis, where they are focusing on isolating specific "mutually exclusive groups" for the purpose of being able to show how the population/community is divided into distinct categories. [18]

Qualitative Data Software

A qualitative data software package makes it easier to analyze transcribed meetings that have been converted into electronic text. There are a handful of these packages on the market. They allow you to quickly analyze transcribed spoken data without laboriously cutting and pasting comments or reading and rereading hours of transcripts. The software permits you to "code," linking a section of the transcript (quote, participant characteristics) with an attribute (gender, location) that can be easily grabbed during a search or query.

As an example, a quote in the transcript from an elderly woman needing wider Handi-Bus steps can have three different attributes (called a "node" by the Nvivo software) coded: "woman," "elderly," and "needing wider Handi-Bus steps." Extensive coding of focus group transcripts allows for a finer grain analysis of the data, while a more general coding of the same transcript will yield a more general analysis. (Of course, the software is only as good as the researcher's coding.) One of the more significant reasons qualitative data analysis software can be extremely helpful to planners is that it can analyze transcript data from one meeting or simultaneously analyze several meetings encompassing the entire research project.

Qualitative software improves the process of analyzing transcribed data in three ways. First, it allows you to quickly summarize public meetings according to coded attributes. Further, it conveniently allows you to search texts for specific relationships. An interesting feature with the Nvivo software is that these searches

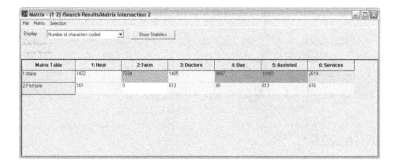

Figure 5.2 Using Nvivo in Qualitative Research

Source: *Using Nvivo in Qualitative Research*, Doncaster, Victoria, Australia: QSR International, 2002, p. 127

can be organized into a qualitative "live" matrix analysis. (See Figure 5.2.) The matrix shown in Figure 5.2 illustrates the pattern of the number of comments per type of group participant ("Male" and "Female"), according to identified research variable (for example, "Services"). If the researcher clicks on the cell below the research variable, for example "Services" and "Male," the software will pull up all the text where male focus group participants talk about rural housing services. Lastly, the software allows you to store all of your transcript data in a single platform where you can analyze multiple transcribed text data in a single analysis.

DISCUSSION QUESTIONS

1. Content analysis is commonly associated with two approaches: Manifest and latent content analysis. Each approach provides a unique insight into your text. Can you see a content analysis research opportunity where you apply both manifest and latent content analysis in a single research project? What would be reasons for you to apply both content analysis approaches?

2. One of the strengths connected with manifest content analysis is that it allows you to quantify qualitative data (words). In what type of planning research situations would it be better for you to go with a latent analysis than a manifest analysis?

3. Semantic internal validity is a particularly vexing problem when conducting a content analysis of community input text on technically complicated planning situations. Sometimes community members do not exactly know the meaning of technical planning terms but are actively talking about them in their comments in public hearings. How do you recognize and reconcile both the definitions of technical terms and community comments that incorrectly use the same terms in public hearing transcripts?

NOTES

i Portions of this discussion appear in Gaber, John. 2000. "Meta-needs assessment," *Evaluation and Program Planning*, 23, pp. 139–147.

ii City of Lincoln, Lincoln City-Lancaster Planning Department. 1998. Change of Zone 3055 S. 14th and Pine Lake Road (map), February 9.

REFERENCES

[1] Kobza, K. 2005. "10 tips for web-based citizen participation," in American Planning Association (ed.), *Planning*, Chicago, IL: American Planning Association, pp. 34–35.

[2] Gray, J., and Densten, I. 1998. "Integrating quantitative and qualitative analysis using latent and manifest variables," *Quality and Quantity*, 32, pp. 419–431, p. 420.

[3] Weber, R. 1990. *Basic Content Analysis* (2nd ed.). Newbury Park, CA: Sage Publications, p. 13.

[4] Budd, R., Thorp, R., and Donohew, L. 1967. *Content Analysis of Communications*. New York: Macmillan, p. 39.

[5] Takahashi, L. and Gaber, S. 1998. "Controversial facility siting in the urban environment: Resident and planner perceptions in the United States", *Environment and Behavior*, 30(2), pp. 184–215.

[6] Weber, *Basic Content Analysis*, p. 44.

[7] Krippendorff, K. 2004. *Content Analysis*. Thousand Oaks, CA: Sage Publications, p. 274.

[8] Hunter, J., and Schmidt, F. 1990. *Methods of Meta-Analysis*. Newbury Park, CA: Sage Publications.

[9] Krippendorff, *Content Analysis*, pp. 319 and 321.

[10] Berg, B. 1998. *Qualitative Research Methods for the Social Sciences* (3rd ed.). Boston, MA: Allyn & Bacon.

[11] Neuendorf, K. 2002. *The Content Analysis Guidebook*. Thousand Oaks, CA: Sage Publications.

[12] Krippendorff, *Content Analysis*, p. 215; Weber, *Basic Content Analysis*, p. 17.

[13] Cukier, K. and Mayer-Schoenberger, V. 2013. "The rise of big data: How it is changing the way we think about the world," *Foreign Affairs*, 92, pp. 28–40, 28.

[14] Dawes, S. S. 2008. "Governance in the information age: A research framework for an uncertain future," *Proceedings of the 9th Annual International Digital Government Conference*, Montréal, pp. 290–297, 290, Linders, P. 2012. "From e-government to we government: Defining a typology for citizen participation in the age of social media," *Government Information Quarterly*, 29(4), 446–454.

[15] Krippendorff, *Content Analysis*, p. 215.

[16] Attewell, P., and Monagha, D. 2015. *Data Mining for the Social Sciences: An Introduction*. Oakland, CA: University of California Press.

[17] Robinson, W., Gordon-Larsen, P., Kaufman, J., Suchindran, C., and Stevens., J. 2009. "The female-male disparity in obesity prevalence among black American young adults: Contributions of socioeconomic characteristics of the childhood family," *American Journal of Clinical Nursing*, 89, pp. 1204–1212.

[18] Lee, S., and Siu, K. 2001. "A review of data mining techniques," *Industrial Management Data Systems*, 101(1), pp. 41–46.

6

GETTING THE BIG PICTURE

THE BIG PICTURE

All planning research begins from the same point of departure: A question. From that point, a planner frames the investigation with a research strategy to address the question. In Chapter 1 I argued that planners should adopt a "paradigm of choice" approach to research methods. The question and the needed data slices to answer the question should be the focus to determine the organization and direction of the investigation. From my experience, I have seen that the research questions a planner faces daily are multifaceted and contain both quantitative and qualitative data slices.

In this book, I have shown how planners can apply four different techniques (field research, photographic investigations, focus group research, and content analysis/meta-analysis) to access qualitative data. By taking a "paradigm of choice" approach, you will quickly realize that many of your research questions can be best addressed through a mixture of both quantitative and qualitative data slices combined into one research project. A mixed method research strategy provides you with a "big picture" understanding of your questions because it incorporates qualitative and quantitative research strategies into the investigation.

This chapter shows how you can get the "big picture" perspective by integrating the qualitative research techniques discussed in this book with quantitative strategies in a mixed method investigation. To achieve this goal, I will define mixed method research, then outline the five most common reasons why planners would be interested in this technique. The five motives for mixed method research investigations are integrated with the four qualitative research techniques discussed in this book into a matrix to show how each method fits in a mixed method research project. This discussion is followed with a brief overview of typical research situations where a planner would use a mixed method study.

Instead of analyzing the mixed method research design in relation to questions of internal and external validity and reliability as I have done in previous chapters, I identify the most common criticisms of mixed method research strategies, all of which fall along the lines of questions of internal validity. I conclude the chapter with two case studies. The first research project looks at the siting of palliative care in British Columbia, Canada, while the second describes a comprehensive housing market study for the state of Nebraska.

WHAT IS MIXED METHOD RESEARCH?

Working in a mixed method investigation requires you to combine more than one research method to generate multiple data slices that are organized into a single research project. Mixed method research projects involve the integration of quantitative methods (the collection of numbers) and qualitative methods (the collection of words and images). Mixed method research is sometimes referred to as triangulation, based on the surveying and nautical process in which two points are used to determine the unknown distance to a third point. [1] An example would be the combination of census data with participant observation field research data to learn more about a particular community.

Mixed method research involves *methodological triangulation*, the use of different methods to analyze a specific situation. [2] Methodological triangulation is one of four types of multiple method research designs. The others are data triangulation, where investigators search for as many different data sources as possible within the same method; investigator triangulation, using multiple observers of the same object; and theory triangulation, the application of multiple perspectives in relation to the same set of objects. The focus of this chapter is on how planners can use methodological triangulation in their research projects.

Mixed method research design is further broken down into two kinds of strategies: *within-method* and *between-method* triangulation. In a within-method investigation, you take one method and use different strategies within it, such as using a survey that asks closed-ended questions for quantitative data and open-ended questions for qualitative data. Between-method investigation combines dissimilar methods to examine a particular situation, such as using census data research and a focus group investigation to figure out the best location for a new neighborhood park. The mixed method research strategies discussed in this chapter are between-method designs.

WHY DO PLANNERS NEED MIXED METHOD RESEARCH?

Mixed method research designs help planners better understand the complexities of life. In most situations, there is not one singular perspective; there are multiple perspectives. Planners are looking out for the public's health, safety, and welfare, as well as for efficiency and equity.

Take the example of the one-way street in Lincoln, Nebraska, in Chapter 4. A single method research strategy (focus group) was used to try to determine how local business owners felt about the conversion of a one-way to a two-way street. That single method study found the business owners were supportive of a two-way street. They felt that two-way traffic would increase their customer base. The city invested in new signs and traffic lights and changed the one-way street to a two-way street. But that is not the end of the story. Less than three months later, the road was converted back to a one-way street. Why? Because this was a situation encompassing multiple interests and competing values. The local business owners were a significant interest group, but the city residents who used the one-way street each day to commute to and from work were not represented in the research process. There was no analysis of the citizens' experiences or feelings about the road conversion. Also, the researchers who did the study never looked at the traffic data for the street. If they had, the vehicle count data would have shown that changing the one-way street to a two-way street would be a bad idea because of existing traffic volume.

Unfortunately, once the conversion was completed, hundreds (more than the total number of business owners that participated in the focus group research) of phone calls to the mayor, city council members, and the planning department pointed to a wide divergence in opinions and the need for a mixed method approach, including traffic data, at the onset. The road is one-way once again.

This example illustrates the need for mixed method research to get a more holistic understanding of complex planning issues. The literature identifies "purposes" (more easily understood as *reasons* why researchers use this technique) for a planner to employ a mixed method research design (see Table 6.1): convergence (triangulation), development, complementarity, expansion, and initiation. [3] *Convergence*, also known in the literature as triangulation, is the most sought after process in mixed method research. The goal is to use several different methods to analyze a single phenomenon in order to increase the validity and credibility of the results. (See Figure 6.1.) But it is actually very difficult to attain. In a mixed method investigation, "each method yields a different picture and slice of reality". [4]

Table 6.1 Five Purposes for Mixed Method Research Strategies

Qualitative Methods	Triangulation	Development
Focus Groups	**Survey analysis** Confirm that data of focus group has validity	**Survey analysis** Develop information to improve survey focus
Windshield Survey	**Census of data analysis** Corroborate that those counted are those living in area	**GIS** To provide additional mapping information
Site Reconnaissance	**Census data analysis** Verify census accurately reflects conditions	**Survey analysis** To improve survey
Complete Observation	**GIS** Convergence of what is mapped	**GIS** Improve sensitivity of existing GIS
Structured/ Semistructured	**Survey analysis** Corroborate survey findings	**Census data** Census data points to what to observe
Unstructured Observations	**Survey analysis** Corroborate survey findings	**Census data** Census data points toward what to observe
Full Participation	**Survey analysis** Corroborate survey findings	**Census data** Census data points toward what to observe
Photographic Mapping	**GIS** Helps correspondence of findings from data	**Census data analysis** Census data corroborate validity of photographic survey
Photographic Survey	**Census data analysis** Census data corroborate validity of photographic survey	**Census Data** Census data points toward what to photograph
Cultural Photographic Inventories	**Survey analysis** Corroborate survey findings	**Survey analysis** To improve survey
Social Process (Photographic)	**Survey analysis** Corroborate survey findings	**Survey analysis** To improve survey
Counting & Measuring (Photographic)	**GIS** Corroborate GIS findings	**Survey analysis** To improve survey focus
Content Analysis	**Survey analysis** Confirmation of survey findings from existing reports	**GIS** Provide new mapping information
Meta-Analysis	**Survey analysis** Confirms survey findings from existing data	**GIS** Provides new mapping information

Complementarity	Expansion	Initiation
Survey analysis Survey for broad information, focus groups for clarity of specifics based on survey	**Community census data analysis** To further understand community beyond census	**Survey analysis** Explore new information uncovered by survey
GIS Add a sense of place to mapping	**Census data analysis** Add depth to data	**Survey analysis** Better observe issue uncovered by survey
Census data analysis Add names/faces to numeric data	**Survey analysis** Extend survey findings	**Census data analysis** Explore information from census data
GIS Improve richness of GIS	**Survey analysis** External breadth of survey findings	**GIS** Initiate new areas for GIS exploration based on observation
GIS Improve richness of GIS	**Census data** Extend breadth of census findings	**GIS** Initiate new areas for GIS exploration
GIS Improve richness of GIS	**Census data** Extend breadth of census findings	**GIS** Initiate new areas for GIS exploration
GIS Improve richness of GIS	**Census data** Extend breadth of census findings	**GIS** Initiate new areas for GIS exploration
GIS Improve richness of aerial photo	**Census data** Extend breadth of photographic findings	**GIS** Initiate further new areas for GIS
Census Data Photos improve richness of census data	**Survey analysis** Extend breadth of survey findings	**Survey analysis** Explore new information covered by photographic survey
Survey analysis Photos improve richness of survey data	**GIS** Further understand community beyond GIS	**Survey analysis** Explore new information found in photos
Survey analysis Photos improve richness of survey data	**GIS** Further understand community beyond GIS	**Survey analysis** Explore new information found in photos
GIS Improve richness of GIS	**Census Data** Extend breadth of photographic data	**GIS** Explore new information in GIS
Census data analysis Adding additional depth of data to numeric data	**Survey analysis** Extend breadth of survey findings	**Census data** Explore new areas identified by census
Census data analysis Adding additional depth of data to numeric data	**Survey analysis** Extend breadth of survey findings	**Census data** Explore new areas identified by census

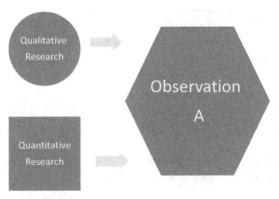

Figure 6.1 Triangulation (Convergence) Mixed Method Research Approach

It is therefore unlikely that two or more methods will come up with the exact same detailed observation. Instead, it is more realistic for the planner to look for different methods to share more general conclusions, for example, the need for more downtown parking, then each method splinters off the shared observation to reveal details that are particularistic to their vista into reality.

Mixed method research strategies can be classified as simultaneous or parallel/sequential. [5] A simultaneous mixed method investigation uses multiple research methods at the same time. In sequential mixed method research, the results of one method are essential for developing the next. Mixing methods for the purpose of *development* involves the sequential use of quantitative and qualitative strategies where results from the first method are used to inform the second method. (See Figure 6.2.) The goal of development is to increase the strength and sensitivity of additional research methods.

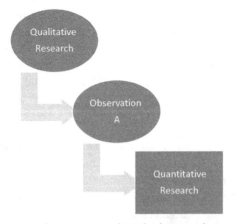

Figure 6.2 Development Mixed Method Research Approach

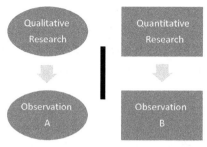

Figure 6.3 Complementarity Mixed Method Research Approach

Complementarity combines methods to measure overlapping, as well as different aspects of a situation, in order to get an enriched enhancement of that situation. (See Figure 6.3.) The goal of complementarity differs from the goal of convergence in that the focus of convergence requires that different methods assess the same conceptual phenomenon, while the methods used in complementarity address different phenomena.

Expansion combines the processes of complementarity and development to extend the range of understanding about a situation by using different methods targeting different components of the situation. Expansion has two goals. (See Figure 6.4.) First, similar to the development process, expansion focuses on applying research methods particularly strong in analyzing specific situations. For example, in an economic development study, the planner may use a survey to analyze local business needs and a traffic count study to look at the number of vehicles that travel through the area. A survey instrument cannot capture a precise understanding of traffic flow as would a traffic count analysis. Information generated from one method is not used to help another method in its assigned tasks. The second goal is similar to the complementarity process—the

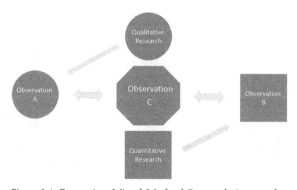

Figure 6.4 Expansion Mixed Method Research Approach

planner applies the images of reality generated by one method to help analyze other sets of images generated by different research methods. Sometimes observations from one study can unexpectedly unfold a new understanding the planner did not anticipate to find in analyzing the results from another investigation in the study.

Initiation is at the opposite end of the mixed method spectrum from convergence. It looks for situations where research findings do not converge. (See Figure 6.5.) The goal of initiation is "to initiate new interpretations, suggest areas for further exploration, or recast the entire research question." [6] Planners use initiation to find sharp contrasts among the data slices. More often than not, however, researchers use an initiation tactic when they are confronted with the dilemma of divergent data. When divergent results emerge, the researcher needs to work as a "builder and creator" in order to resolve the resulting "empirical puzzle." [7]

A new application in mixed method research is planners integrating multiple mixed method approaches (e.g. convergence and expansion) in a single study. [8] Called a "fully integrated" strategy, it is the most complicated mixed method purpose because it requires you to be acutely aware of the different purposes of mixed method investigations and that you are combining two or more purposes to achieve either a more detailed analysis or greater depth of confidence. [9] One of the benefits associated with the fully integrated approach is that it provides you with the opportunity to learn and adjust the focus of your study as it unfolds in the community. For example, while conducting a development mixed research project you uncover a new realization from the focus group section of your research and decide to add a completely new research direction through an initiation investigation.

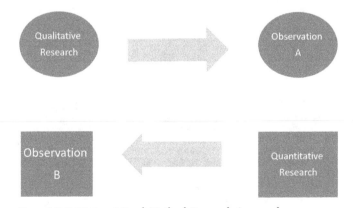

Figure 6.5 Initiation Mixed Method Research Approach

WHEN DO PLANNERS USE MIXED METHOD RESEARCH?

Planners employ mixed method research strategies to get a big-picture answer to their research questions. These types of questions tend to require a mixture of quantitative and qualitative data slices. A multifaceted problem usually includes a combination of substantive topics such as transportation, environment, economics; populations (local residents, businesses owners); geographic territories such as downstream communities, businesses across the street, and a nearby floodplain; and organizations (city, county, regional, state, federal, and international government agencies).

Confronted with a multifaceted problem, a planner armed with a single research method like a survey will simply not generate enough data to adequately address the question at hand, no matter how extensively the research method is applied. I argue that, by the very nature of what planners do on a daily basis, the comprehensive and intricately woven nature of planning makes all planning research projects mixed method in orientation.

DOING MIXED METHOD RESEARCH

Setting Up

Research methodology is very much a design process. [10] As discussed previously in Chapter 1, you need to conceptualize how the five elements of the research act (the question, accessing data, analyzing data, testing the significance of the data, and presenting the research results) will all come together before you actually go out and do the work. In a mixed method research investigation, you are looking at how multiple data slices can answer your research question. At this point in the research project, you need to determine how the varying data slices relate to each other.

Table 6.1 illustrates how the qualitative methods identified in the previous chapters work with quantitative methods for a mixed method design. The table provides examples of methods that might be used together and indicates how these methods work to achieve each of the five purposes of mixed method design.

In a mixed method research design, a data slice can be understood as having one of three relationships to the others. Table 6.2 identifies how to match a research purpose to a type of data. The most easily identifiable data slices are single-faceted. These denote a stand-alone slice of data that can be easily isolated from others. For example, data that answer the question of how many people live in the community is a single-faceted data slice you can obtain through census documents.

Table 6.2 Mixed Method Research Design: Matching Research Purposes to Type of Data Slice

Type of Data Slice	Data Slice Characteristics	Type of Mixed Method Research Design
Single-faceted	A stand-alone slice of data that does not have an obvious relationship to other data slices in the research project	a) Convergence: Using a mixed method research design to increase confidence that observation is confirmed by other data slices
Interconnected	Identified data slices have an obvious interwoven or overlapping relationship to other data slices; the slices of data cannot be completely understood on their own	b) Complementarity: Looking for the overlapping and non-overlapping relationship among identified data slices
Disparate	Single-faceted data slices that lack a clear relationship but are connected to each other by a theoretical or methodological framework	a) Development: Seeing various data slices as stepping stones to develop new methods to access new data slices b) Expansion: Using the observations from one data slice to better understand another data slice c) Initiation: Seeing the disparate data slices as part of an "empirical puzzle" that needs more research to be solved

Use a convergence mixed method approach to obtain and analyze single-faceted data by using more than one method to generate the same type of data slice, such as using both a survey and focus group research to confirm what local residents think about a proposed project in their community.

Interconnected data slices have an interdependent relationship to each other. When one data slice cannot be completely understood on its own and must be seen in its relationship to others to make sense, the slices are interconnected. For example, if you are looking at traffic flow data, you must also analyze land use data to determine how land use and density impact traffic flow.

As you look at interconnected data slices, take a complementarity approach to investigate the overlapping and non-overlapping characteristics among the various data slices. An example of this is looking at data on abandoned buildings and photographic research data to assess the degree and conditions of a deteriorating industrial section of town.

Disparate data slices are single-faceted slices of data connected through either a theoretical or methodological framework. For example, an economic study of a community will examine population census data, land use data, and economic data, among others. All of these data slices are single-faceted by themselves, but together provide a good economic profile of a community.

In addition, you can address a mixed method research design with disparate data slices through three different approaches. The first is to place the data slices in sequential order. In this case, you will use a development design and use another to generate data; you can use the analysis of this data to develop another research method to assess another data slice.

Another approach is to see the data slices as being different from each other, but with each providing added insight for the others. This is an expansion mixed method research strategy. Finally, you can see the data slices as completely divergent. When data slices seem to be scattered in different directions, you will use an initiation research design to try to make sense out of the "empirical puzzle."

Mixed method research projects tend to either be dominant qualitative/less dominant quantitative (big Q and small q) or the reverse. [11] In a Qualitative/quantitative (QUAL + quan) research study, you start the research with a more open-ended, qualitative research approach such as a focus group or photographic research, then use those observations to design or inform additional quantitative research such as a survey. [12]

In a Quantitative/qualitative (QUAN + qual) research strategy, your work will be driven by a structured quantitative framework. This type of research project focuses on quantitative research, such as the survey mentioned above, but then embeds qualitative research within the quantitative research by adding open-ended questions or employs qualitative methods to explore unexpected findings. [13]

Getting the Data

Deciding when different methods are applied in a mixed method research project is largely a function of organizational constraints more than methodological requirements. The only exception is in the case of a development mixed method project. Here, the sequencing of the different methods is paramount because one method must be completed before the second method can be developed.

Organizing the Data

How you organize data slices in a mixed method research project depends on the research methods that were used to retrieve them. Mixed method investigations function as a methodological framework to help you organize a multiple method, multiple data slice research project.

Analyzing the Data

First, analyze the data slices within the research methods that obtained them. For example, you should first analyze the field research observation data before using the results to develop a survey investigation. Once you have finished analyzing all of the data slices in the project, apply convergence, development, complementarity, expansion, and initiation. These five purposes are strategies you can use to organize the different data slices to see how they relate. The various relationships between the data slices (for example, expansion) allow you to get the bigger picture understanding of the research project. To get a clearer idea of how this happens in a real-world situation, see the examples in the case studies at the end of this chapter.

Mixed method research strategies do not need to adhere to a single purpose for triangulation. One mixed method investigation can triangulate its data for more than one purpose. For example, data that are used to develop another research method can also be used for expansion to help you better understand the observations made from a third data slice. The multiple combinations of different mixed method research strategies are illustrated in the case study of free flow right-hand turn lanes later in this chapter.

QUESTIONS OF VALIDITY AND RELIABILITY IN MIXED METHOD RESEARCH

Unique to mixed method research design is the growing interest in the "validating or quality criteria in mixed method" research projects. [14] One of the added challenges in mixed method research projects is that the planner needs to address questions of external and internal validity per research project (e.g. focus group and photographic investigation) as well as address "validity" or what mixed method researchers call "legitimation" questions associated with the chosen mixed method approach (e.g. convergence). [15] Although still in the early stages of development, recent work by Onwuegbuzzie and Johnson has created a typology of nine mixed method "legitimation types" (sample integration, inside-outside, weakness minimization, sequential, conversion, paradigmatic mixing, commensurability, multiple validities, and political) which the planner can use to assess the quality of her mixed method observations. (See Table 6.3.)

Table 6.3 Typology of Mixed Methods Legitimation Types

Legitimation Type	Description	Type of Validity
Sample Integration	The extent to which the relationship between the quantitative and qualitative sample design yields quality meta-inferences	External Validity
Inside-Outside	The extent to which the researcher accurately presents and appropriately utilizes the insider's view and the observer's view for purposes such as description and explanation	Internal Validity
Weakness Minimization	The extent to which the weakness from one approach is compensated by the strengths from the other approach	Internal Validity
Sequential	The extent to which one has minimized the potential problem wherein the meta-inferences could be affected by reversing the sequences of the quantitative and qualitative phases	Internal Validity
Conversion	The extent to which the quantitizing or qualitizing yields meta-inferences	Internal Validity
Paradigmatic Mixing	The extent to which the researcher's epistemological, ontological, axiological, methodological, and rhetorical beliefs that underlie the quantitative and qualitative approaches are successfully (a) combined or (b) blended into a usable package	Internal and External Validity
Commensurability	The extent to which the meta-inferences made reflect a mixed worldview based on the cognitive process of Gestalt switching and integration	Internal Validity
Multiple Validities	The extent to which addressing legitimation of the quantitative and qualitative components of the study result from the use of quantitative, qualitative, and mixed validity types, yielding high-quality meta-inferences	Internal and External Validity
Political/ Professional Claim	The extent to which the consumer of mixed methods research value the meta-inferences stemming from both the quantitative and qualitative components of a study	No Validity

Sample Integration Legitimation

This legitimation concern focuses on external validity and the ability of the planner to generalize her observations to a larger population. "Unless exactly the same individuals or groups of individuals are involved in both the qualitative and quantitative components of a study, constructing meta-inferences by pulling together the inferences from the qualitative and quantitative phases can be problematic." [16] This legitimation question mostly focuses on qualitative research projects and looks at the planner's sampling process in terms of who was contacted and how many individuals were in the sampled population in relation to the quantitative study. It is important to point out that questions regarding sample integration only focus on mixed method research projects when the planner is comparing quantitative and qualitative population-specific data slices (e.g. focus group data and survey data) and not research projects when the investigator integrates a quantitative population specific data slice (e.g. survey data) with a non-population specific qualitative data slice (e.g. photographic research).

The real-life limitations inherent in the planning research context sometimes prevent the planner from being able to increase their qualitative research sample size so it is comparable to their quantitative research project. Although limited in their generalizability, statistically underrepresentative qualitative research observations are critically important to the investigator in contributing to their obtaining a clearer holistic understanding of the planning problem at hand. There are two ways the planner can address sample integration legitimation questions when they have a smaller sampled qualitative investigation in relation to their quantitative study. First, you accept and document your smaller qualitative project and then, instead of making empirical generalizations to the larger community, you make theoretical observations to the larger community. This is done by framing your qualitative observations (e.g. focus group) in a larger theoretical framework and having them speak to your quantitative observations and the larger community in general terms rather than in a predictive sense. [17]

The second option in addressing concerns of sample integration is for the planner to place their qualitative observations within a range of observations in relation to their quantitative observations. The bracketing of observations is commonly applied in meta-analysis investigations where the planner combines multiple secondary data sources, some of which come from smaller sampled studies than others. Pluye et al. "suggest a scoring system to concomitantly appraise the methodological quality of qualitative, quantitative and mixed method studies." [18] The scoring system allows you to fully integrate your statistically less significant quantitative investigations with your quantitative data, but lets the reader know upfront that the quantitative data comes from a smaller sampled population that limits the amount of confidence you have in your qualitative observations.

Insider-Outsider Legitimation

The insider-outsider legitimation question is an internal validity question and looks at whether the planner captured the representative "community's view" in her mixed method research project. This legitimation question is based on the representation of the community's view as possessing a particular ontological perspective toward reality with it being either from an "insider perspective" (called an emic view) provided by local residents and their lived experiences or an "outsider perspective" (called an etic view) which is made up of "experts" who know a lot about the emic community members.

The planner needs to be cognizant of two types of inside-outsider legitimation questions. The first question looks to see if the planner actually captured an emic view by only sampling local residents in their study. If not, the planner may be reporting that they captured an "insider" community's perspective in their study, when in reality they actually got more of an etic "outsider" perspective from local experts. Using etic sampled experts who are providing their understanding of the "community's view" "runs the risk of legitimizing a decision in which a substantial proportion of the (actual) community have not been involved despite the assessment being conducted under the banner of 'participation'." [19] To answer this insider-outsider legitimation question, you need to clearly document who in the community you contacted and to identify if any of the interviewed residents belong to any organized interests that may sway their observations toward a particular agenda.

The second question evaluates the mixed method approach to see if the planner has chosen the most appropriate research technique (e.g. focus group research) to obtain emic and etic observations. As pointed out in Chapter 1, some research techniques are better at getting qualitative data while others are better at obtaining qualitative data. "Quantitative research (e.g. survey) often seeks the objective outsider view (and) qualitative research (e.g. focus group research) often seeks the insider's view, and mixed research seeks to balance fully these two viewpoints." [20] In practice, the planner does not always correctly apply the most appropriate research technique (e.g. interviews) per desired community perspective and often applies quantitative research strategies to obtain emic community perspectives and sometimes applies qualitative research techniques to obtain etic observations. The problem with the planner applying quantitative research strategies to obtain qualitative observations from the local community is that the thick descriptive emic observations are significantly curtailed and are slotted into simple antiseptic statistical data slices. The only way you can address the second question of insider-outsider legitimation is to apply the appropriate qualitative research strategies when you are seeking to capture the community's insider perspective.

Weakness Minimization Legitimation

One of the main reasons why the planner takes to a mixed method research approach is to be able to compensate for the weakness in one research technique (e.g. qualitative interviews) with the strengths of a different research technique (e.g. GIS). The weakness minimization legitimation question looks at how well the planners "assess the extent to which the weakness from one approach can be compensated by the strengths from the other approach." [21] This legitimation assessment is an internal validity question and focuses on the appropriateness of the planner conclusions when she uses one research technique to compensate for the weaknesses in another technique. The best way the planner can address the weakness minimization legitimation claim is to carefully document the strength and weaknesses in each research technique used in their mixed method investigation and show how their observations are drawn from the complementarity relationship between the two (or more) methods.

Sequential Legitimation

The question of sequential legitimation excludes sequential mixed method projects for development (results from one study to help develop the research tool for a second study) and instead focuses on those investigations where the planner sequentially applies expansion and fully integrated multi-method projects. This internal validity question analyzes the planner's final mixed method conclusions and looks for the possibility that she arrived at these observations as a function of the sequencing of methods onto themselves instead of through the integration of quantitative and qualitative observations. The concern here is that the research process in itself created an inertia of observations where the addition of each new research project resulted in the continuation of the observations from the previous research projects. The way the sequential legitimation problem can be spotted is by looking to see "if the results and interpretations would have been different if the order of the quantitative and qualitative phases originally presented had been reversed". [22] One way the planner can guard themselves from sequential legitimation problems is by periodically switching the timing of individual qualitative and quantitative research projects to prevent the development of an inertial effect so one set of research observations does not set the tone over other research observations.

Conversion Legitimation

Sometimes a planner in the data analysis stage of a mixed method research project will transform one type of data (qualitative or quantitative) and analyze it as another type of data. Conversion legitimation is an internal validity assessment and looks at the appropriateness of converting one data type into a different data type and the observations the planner derives from this conversion. The planner can either "quantitize" their qualitative data and convert them to quantitative data or they can "qualitize" their quantitative data and analyze them as qualitative data. One problem in the planner utilizing a quantitize conversion analysis is that counting may not be appropriate for some qualitative slices. This may result in the planner overcounting or out-of-context counting qualitative data, which leads to research conclusions that are not founded in the reality of the qualitative data. On the other side of the data conversion spectrum, some qualitative data slices are not easily converted by the planner into quantitative data. "A common method of qualitizing data is via narrative profile formation" which requires the planner to construct "narrative descriptions from quantitative data". [23] Quantitative data that defies qualitizing may result in the planner either over-generalizing the quantitative data and glossing over statistically significant variances in the data or stereotyping a grouping of statistical data and developing a profile of people that does not exist in the community.

Paradigmatic Mixing Legitimation

This legitimation question is leveled at the entire mixed method approach and argues that any conclusion the planner derives from their mixed method project should be both internally and externally invalid. This position is taken at the large-scale paradigm level and sees that scientific quantitative data slices and naturalistic qualitative data cannot be mixed in a single research project because they each look at empirical reality differently. Guba and Lincoln state that the mixing of quantitative and qualitative data "is logically equivalent to calling for a compromise between the view that the world is flat and the view the world is round." [24] There is nothing the planner can do to fix their mixed method research project to address the concern on the paradigmatic mixing legitimation question. In response to Guba and Lincoln's assertion is the "situationalist" counter-argument. The situationalists contend that paradigmatic distinctions are important, but researchers can be "flexible" in making decisions that are appropriate to particular research situations. The planner should opt for a "paradigm of choices," which contains the recognition that different methods are appropriate for different situations. Understanding the epistemological differences between different research methods helps to make the planner more aware of methodological biases "so that [she] can [emphasis in original] make flexible, sophisticated, and adaptive methodological choices." [25]

Commensurability Legitimation

The commensurability legitimation question mirrors the paradigmatic mixing legitimation assessment in that it does not think the planner can successfully execute a mixed method research project. This legitimation question argues that quantitative and qualitative research projects are holistically autonomous research acts that cannot be broken down into smaller working components that can be combined with other different research projects. [26] The commensurability legitimation question is an internal validity question in that it questions the meta-inferences the planner makes among their quantitative and qualitative investigations. Again, similar to how the planner addresses the paradigmatic mixing legitimation question, she needs to clearly define the research problem as being multifaceted in nature and that the uniqueness inherent in quantitative and qualitative research strategies allows her to reach a more holistic understanding of the situation at hand.

Multiple Validities Legitimation

Mixed method research is more challenging than single method research strategies because the planner needs to be cognizant of more internal validity threats than if they only applied a single research technique. This legitimation type "refers to the extent to which all relevant research strategies are utilized and the research can be considered high on multiple relevant 'validities'." [27] The best way the planner addresses the multiple variables legitimation question is to line-item each external and internal validity concern you have per research technique and identify each action you take to mitigate the "trade-offs" you had to take to ensure validity in each research technique.

Sometimes, if the planner does not take the necessary measures to protect each research project from questions of internal validity in their mixed method investigation, they may experience intra-method internal validity problems. This most commonly can occur in convergence mixed method research and it is called "pseudo-convergence." Pseudo-convergence is when a planner has two or more methods producing shared observations, but the investigator is unable to rule out one or both methods being biased in the same "wrong" direction. [28] One solution to the problems associated with methodological bias in mixed method investigations is to shift the focus on triangulation away from convergence and validity, and concentrate instead on using mixed methods to construct plausible explanations through the expansion process. However, ignoring the goal of convergence still does not solve the problem of "pseudo-convergence," when different methods yield similar results. The only possible way to stay clear of this potential shortfall is to make sure that the methods you use are very focused on capturing a desired "data slice." Any poorly focused method in a mixed method research project not only increases the suspicion of that particular method, but also throws the other methods used under suspicion of "pseudo-convergence."

Political/Professional Legitimation

This legitimation concern does not have any connection to questions of external and internal validity and refers to some of the political and professional tensions associated with the planner applying a mixed method investigation. Planners work with different professions (architects, engineers, health professionals, etc.) on a daily basis to address shared problems in the community.

> These tensions include any value or ideologically based conflicts that occur when different researchers are used for the quantitative and qualitative phases of a study, as well as differences in perspectives about contradictions and paradoxes that arise when the quantitative and qualitative findings are compared and contrasted. [29]

CASE STUDY #1: SITING PALLIATIVE CARE IN BRITISH COLUMBIA, CANADA

Crooks et al.'s study of siting palliative care services in rural British Columbia (BC), Canada, is one example of an integrative expansion mixed method research project. [30] Rural Canada is vast with huge distances between communities.

Confronted with the growing need for the provision of care for people at the end stages of life (palliative care) in rural areas, the investigator focused on the siting of secondary palliative care hubs (SPCH) to improve the availability of appropriate medical care. SPCHs are the coordination of palliative services for rural residents who do not have access to a residential hospice.

The researchers began their investigation with a standard quantitative "suitability" location analysis model. The factors included in this model included: the total population within an hour of the community (where larger populations are more suitable), the vulnerability of the community calculated as the total population 65 years and older in the one-hour area (where larger populations are more suitable), and the isolation of the community as measured by travel time to the nearest specialized palliative care facility (where longer travel times to existing facilities are more suitable). [31] The results from the quantitative study provided observations about rural communities that were the most "suitable" for SPCH services.

The quantitative suitability analysis was followed by qualitative investigation with palliative care service providers. Here, the researchers conducted 31 interviews from a purposefully sampled group of formal and informal palliative care providers in the rural interior area known as the West Kootenay-Boundary region. The goal of the interviews was to identify barriers and facilitators to palliative care service delivery as a way to test their responsiveness to an SPCH service system. Participants were asked questions that focused on community health care priorities and challenges, experience with palliative care, availability of palliative care services and anticipated future need, and knowledge about the SPCH approach. Interviews were transcribed and thematically analyzed according to a pattern investigation analysis. The interview data opened up a new level of complexity beyond their first quantitative analysis and identified "community readiness" as a key factor for the siting of SPCHs in needy rural communities. The researchers identified five variables related to community readiness: (a) community awareness, (b) training and education, (c) telemedicine utilization, (d) presence of family doctors, and (e) community momentum. [32]

The qualitative findings dramatically changed how the researchers understood their original quantitative analysis and decided to recalculate their suitability siting model by integrating the qualitative interview "readiness" findings. This required the researchers to convert the five "readiness" qualitative themes into quantitative binary yes/no indicators (see Table 6.4). The addition of the five community readiness variables and their associated

Table 6.4 Community Readiness Variables and Indicators

Variable	Meaning	Binary Indicator (Y/N)
Community Awareness	Palliative care is not always thought of as a priority issue. Does palliative care have visibility or a "profile" in the community?	Is there a local hospice society (as these groups play a major role in local advocacy)?
Training and Education	Participants made it clear that strengthening palliative care in rural and remote communities would require providing local educational opportunities. Thus, is there a site to host and possibly coordinate such initiatives?	Is there a local college or university campus?
Telemedicine Utilization	Telemedicine can increase capacity for providing palliative care in smaller sites. Is the community ready to link larger centers via telemedicine in order to facilitate information sharing?	Is there regular use of telemedicine at the local hospital?
Presence of Family Doctor	Family doctors play a vital role in providing palliative care in rural areas. Are there adequate family medicine resources available locally in order to enhance palliative care provision?	Do family doctors practicing locally have an adequate family physician to population ratio?
Momentum	Enhancing palliative care was not seen as an end point, but rather the start of accomplishing larger goals, such as the development of a hospice house. Has there been a demonstration by the community of the desire to increase palliative care capacity?	Has a proposal been put forth to create a local hospice?

indicators to the original suitability SPCH quantitative siting model provided further confirmation for the top six suitable communities as having high readiness to receive SPCH services. However, the new suitability/readiness analysis did rearrange the researchers' ranking of middle- and bottom-tier communities, causing some communities now to be recognized as noticeably more suitable and others less suitable.

CASE STUDY #2: NEBRASKA HOUSING MARKET STUDY

Mixed method research design is particularly adept at dealing with very large and complicated investigations. We were asked by the Nebraska Department of Economic Development (DED) to lead a team of seven researchers, including ourselves, to conduct a comprehensive housing market study for the entire state. [33] The goal was to assess the supply and demand for housing and, particularly, the supply and need for affordable, decent, safe, and sanitary housing for low-income residents. DED gave us three questions it wanted data to address:

> SUPPLY: What housing stock and housing programs existed in Nebraska?
>
> DEMAND: What housing stock and programs were needed?
>
> SOLUTIONS: What can be done to meet the housing needs?

We used a complementarity mixed method research approach to implement and coordinate the 12 different research projects in the study. The separate research strategies were connected to each question as follows:

Supply: What housing stock and housing programs currently exist in Nebraska?

1. Meta-analysis of comprehensive plans and housing studies completed for cities and counties in Nebraska between 1995 and 2000.
2. Summarize existing housing programs or policies for specific populations (for example, migrant workers).
3. Mail survey to 532 municipalities regarding housing stock needs.
4. Obtain building permit data in all county tax assessor offices.
5. Phone interviews with nonprofit and for-profit housing program agencies.
6. Obtain data from regional representatives from the Nebraska Board of Realtors.

Demand: What housing stock and programs were needed?

1. Conduct 14 focus group meetings throughout the state to identify barriers and con-straints to housing and housing-related services for special needs populations.
2. Mail survey to chambers of commerce throughout the state to determine housing and perceived housing demand in relation to Target Industry study.

Solutions: What can be done to meet the housing needs?

1. Mail survey sent to the 124 home builders across the state to identify measures that can mitigate housing problems.
2. Mail survey sent to 157 banks, mortgage companies, credit unions, and savings and loans that provide mortgages to identify barriers and ways to overcome barriers to affordable housing in the state.
3. Analyze outstanding and innovative model housing programs used in other states.

Given the size and scope of the study, we divided the planning recommendations according to the three primary regions of the state (east, central, and west) and specific process-oriented housing topics.

For the regional recommendations, all the data that focused on the region, county, or town within one of the three regions were put into a Housing Market Synthesis matrix. (See Table 6.5.) The synthesis matrix allowed the DED staff to easily see how the different data slices spoke to each region in the state and how the different regions compared to each other. Note how the combination of quantitative data in the "Building Permits" column with the qualitative data in the "Special Populations" column shows how the western part of the state is struggling more with rural housing needs (migrant housing) and has a smaller housing stock (the highest number of building permits issued was 1,196, in Lincoln County), while the central part of the state is facing more urban housing needs (homelessness) and has a much larger housing stock (Douglas County issued 28,899 permits).

When working on a large-scale project like this one, it is easy to fail the test of external validity by generalizing your observations beyond your data. We knew, for example, that it was not realistic to generalize the data from the 14 focus groups past their geographic region. To avoid being vulnerable to questions of external validity, we generalized the focus group data at the policy level and used the thick descriptions from the community to address specific housing issues in the state.

Our conclusion identified 10 recommendations that focused on process-oriented housing topics. The assumption here was that, as a state agency, DED could have more influence on removing barriers in the process of providing affordable housing than with its actual construction. Within each recommendation we connected our observation to data slices that supported our claim. Below are three examples that were written in the final report.

Table 6.5 Nebraska Housing Market Study Synthesis by Regions

Regions	Meta-Analysis of Special Populations	Municipalities Survey	Building-Permits 1998–2000
Western	Northwest needs migrant labor housing (144–180 units needed over next 12 years). Southwest has limited housing services available.	Northwest cited too much poor, dilapidated housing. Southwest cited lack of affordable rentals and homes for sale for low-income populations. Southwest has lowest occupancy rate (90.3). Both areas cited lack of middle-income housing for sale and affordable rentals.	**Northwest:** Box Butte Co. 98 Dawson Co. 615 Lincoln Co. 1,196 Sheridan Co. 37 **Southwest:** Chase Co. 99 Gosper Co. 75 Red Willow Co. 236
Central	South Central needs transitional facilities and low-income housing	South Central cited a lack of affordable rental housing for low and middle-income populations. North Central cited too much poor, dilapidated housing. North Central has highest average owner occupied rate (87.2%). Both areas cited lack of middle-income housing for sale and affordable rentals.	**South Central:** Adams Co. 1,177 Buffalo Co. 2,791 Clay Co. 144 Hall Co. 2,300 **North Central:** Antelope Co. 165 Cherry Co. 104 Holt Co. 160 Knox Co. 277 Loup Co. 2

Regions	Meta-Analysis of Special Populations	Municipalities Survey	Building-Permits 1998–2000
Eastern	Southeast (City of Lincoln) needs 289 units for homeless and other special populations. Northeast has greatest need on reservations and City of Omaha needs units for persons with HIV/AIDS.	Southeast cited a lack of affordable rental housing for low-income populations. Northeast has highest occupancy rate (95.8%). Both areas cited lack of middle-income housing for sale and affordable rentals.	**Southeast:** Cass Co. 1,750 Lancaster Co. 20,596 Sarpy Co. 12,355 Saunders Co. 841 **Northeast:** Burt Co. 136 Cedar Co. 122 Douglas Co. 28,899 Madison Co. 1,669 Platte Co. 1,282 Polk Co. 66 Washington Co. 1,540

Training for Skilled Labor to Work in Housing Industry

Many of the survey respondents (municipalities, builders, and lenders) indicated that there was a shortage of skilled labor to work in the housing construction industry, both in new construction and in rehabs. Without an improved supply of labor in this area, it will be difficult to increase housing availability and meet housing needs.

Lenders Don't Want to Lend on Speculation Housing

Low-income housing needs to be helped from the public side. From the lenders survey, it became clear that they were apprehensive about providing loans on speculative housing. This means that little speculation housing was being created, particularly outside of the metropolitan areas. The implication of this was that low-income housing needed to have public (government) support if it is to get built. Few low-income people can afford to pay to have housing built.

Educate Communities on Availability of Funds

The chamber of commerce survey pointed out that many communities are unaware of some of the basic housing assistance programs. Further education about housing programs, particularly in conjunction with the chambers of commerce, seemed worthwhile. According to the chamber survey, housing is an important component of economic development.

DISCUSSION QUESTIONS

1. It is widely accepted that the mixed method research approach allows the planner to generate a more holistic understanding of the planning problem at hand. Are more data slices always better in planning? Provide a real-life planning situation where a mixed method research approach is needed to adequately capture the complexities of what is going on in the community. Next, provide an example where a mixed method research project would be unnecessary and detrimental to the overall planning effort.

2. The mixed method research approach is a multi-method research strategy that combines quantitative and qualitative data slices. Can you use the five mixed method research approaches (triangulation (convergence), development, complementarity, expansion, and initiation) in a multi-method quantitative or qualitative research project? If so, how would you do it for a multi-method quantitative project? And for a multi-method qualitative project? Are the same "legitimation" validity questions that are used to assess mixed method projects applicable to mono-approach multi-method projects?

3. Mixed method research projects are very creative in that they allow the planner to tailor their research effort to the specific community planning needs they are facing. The uniqueness of planning and public policy mixed method research projects comes at the expense of them being easily replicated by other planning researchers who are facing similar community planning situations. Is the lack of replicability of planning mixed method research a problem in the advancement of planning and public policy research in general? If so, how? And should future planning mixed method research projects be more quantitatively oriented (QUAN-qual) to provide more opportunities for replication of research projects in the future?

REFERENCES

[1] Tashakkori, A., and Teddlie, C. 1998. *Mixed Methodology: Combining Qualitative and Quantitative Approaches.* Thousand Oaks, CA: Sage Publications, p. 41.

[2] Denzin, N. 1989. *The Research Act: A Theoretical Introduction to Sociological Methods* (3rd ed.). Englewood Cliffs, NJ: Prentice-Hall, p. 237.

[3] Greene, J., Caracellie, V., and Graham, W. 1989. "Toward a conceptual framework for mixed-method evaluation design," *Educational Evaluation and Policy Analysis,* 11(3), pp. 255–274; Greene, Jennifer and Charles McClintock. 1985. "Triangulation in evaluation: Design and analysis issues," *Evaluation Review,* 9(5), pp. 523–545.

[4] Denzin, *Research Act,* p. 256.

[5] Tashakkori and Teddlie, *Mixed Methodology,* pp. 46–47.

[6] Rossman, G., and Wilson, B. 1985. "Numbers and words: Combining quantitative and qualitative methods in a single large-scale evaluation study," *Evaluation Review,* 9(5), p. 635.

[7] Jick, T. 1983. "Mixing qualitative and quantitative methods: Triangulation in action," in *Qualitative Methodology.* edited by J. Van Maanen. Beverly Hills, CA: Sage Publications, p. 144.

[8] Tashakkori and Teddlie, *Mixed Methodology,* p. 156.

[9] Gaber, J., and Overacker, T. 2012. "Establishing mixed method research design guidelines in health impact assessment investigations," *Impact Assessment and Project Appraisal,* 30(4), pp. 275–283, p. 280.

[10] Creswell, J. 1994. *Research Design: Qualitative and Quantitative Approaches.* Thousand Oaks, CA: Sage Publications.

[11] Morse, J. 1991. "Approaches to qualitative-quantitative methodological triangulation," *Nursing Research,* 40(2), p. 120; Creswell, 1994, p. 177.

[12] Tashakkori and Teddlie, *Mixed Methodology,* p. 47.

[13] Morse, "Approaches," p. 121.

[14] Onwuegbuzie, A., and Johnson, B. 2006. "The validity issue in mixed research," *Research in the Schools,* 13(1), pp. 48–63, p. 55.

[15] Collins, K., Onwuegbuzie, A., and Jiao, Q. 2007. "A mixed method investigation of mixed methods sampling designs in social and health science research," *Journal of Mixed Methods Research,* 1(3), pp. 267–294.

[16] Onwuegbuzie and Johnson, "The validity issue," p. 56.

[17] Yin, R. 1994. *Case Study Research: Design and Methods* (2nd ed.). Thousand Oaks, CA, Sage Publications, p. 37.

[18] Pluye, P., Gagnon, M., Griffiths, F., and Johson-Lafleur, J. 2009. "A scoring system for appraising mixed methods research, and concomitantly appraising qualitative, quantitative and mixed methods primary studies in mixed studies reviews," *International Journal of Nursing Studies*, 46, pp. 529–546.

[19] Maheswaran, D., and Shavitt, S. 2000. "Issues and new directions in global consumer psychology," *Journal of Consumer Psychology*, 9(2), 59–66.

[20] Onwuegbuzie and Johnson, "The validity issue," p. 58.

[21] Onwuegbuzie and Johnson, "The validity issue," p. 58.

[22] Onwuegbuzie and Johnson, "The validity issue," p. 58.

[23] Onwuegbuzie and Johnson, "The validity issue," p. 59.

[24] Guba, E., and Lincoln, Y. 1998. "Do inquiry paradigms imply inquiry methodologies," in *Qualitative Approaches to Evaluation Education*, edited by D. Fetterman. New York: Praeger, pp. 89–115.

[25] Patton, M. 1998. "Paradigms and Pragmatism," in *Qualitative Approaches to Evaluation and Education: The Silent Revolution*, edited by L. Shortland and M. Mark. San Francisco, CA: Jossey-Bass, p. 81.

[26] Chen, X. 1997. "Thomas Kuhn's latest notion of incommensurability," *Journal of General Philosophy of Science*, 28(2), pp. 257–273, p. 258.

[27] Onwuegbuzie and Johnson, "The validity issue," p. 59.

[28] Shortland, L., and Mark, M. 1987. "Improving inference from multiple methods," in *Multiple Methods in Program Evaluation*, edited by L. Shortland and M. Mark. San Francisco, CA: Jossey-Bass, p. 81.

[29] Onwuegbuzie and Johnson, "The validity issue," p. 59.

[30] Crooks, V., Schuurman, N., Cinnamon, J., Castleden, H., and Johnston, R. 2011. "Refining a location analysis model using a mixed methods approach: Community readiness as a key factor in the siting rural palliative care services," *Journal of Mixed Methods Research*, 5(1), pp. 77–95.

[31] Crooks et al., "Refining a location analysis model," p. 80.

[32] Crooks et al., "Refining a location analysis model," p. 82.

[33] Center for Applied Research (CARI). 2001. *Nebraska Housing Study*. Lincoln, NB: University of Nebraska.

7

APPLYING QUALITATIVE TECHNIQUES IN CITIZEN PARTICIPATION

HOW ARE QUALITATIVE TECHNIQUES USED IN CITIZEN PARTICIPATION?

Qualitative research techniques are commonly used by planners in their citizen participation projects. Citizen participation is a critical step in the plan-making process and is when planners integrate multiple community perspectives in the development and assessment of plans and public policies to make them more relevant and representative of those who are impacted by them. Sherry Arnstein defines citizen participation as "the redistribution of power that enables the have-not citizens, presently excluded from the political and economic process, to be deliberately included in the future." [1] The exploratory and community-based nature inherent to qualitative research techniques makes them useful tools for planners to systematically engage targeted segments of the community and provide alternative ways to record and analyze their lived experiences.

WHY DO PLANNERS AND POLICY MAKERS APPLY QUALITATIVE METHODS IN CITIZEN PARTICIPATION?

Planners use qualitative techniques in their citizen participation projects for one of three purposes. First, planners use qualitative techniques when they seek multiple community perspectives as guidance for developing policy and optimizing the implementation of plans and projects. [2] Qualitative research strategies are particularly useful when planners have to generate observations from a select group of key informants and record their observations as they relate to the planning problem at hand. When the planner accesses multiple areas of expertise inside and outside of the affected community, community input can make the policy more sensitive to local experiences. For example, a city planning office looking to expand the width of a bridge that goes over an ecologically sensitive wetland may seek advice from a wildlife biologist, hydrologist, and traffic engineer before formally developing their bridge widening plan.

Second, planners use qualitative techniques to access community input for the purpose of generating data slices as part of their qualitative research projects. The foundation to community empirical observations is Dewey's "postulate of immediate empiricism" where the community is understood as being able to provide empirical "non-technical observations" on "everyday things" that they experience in their day-to-day lives. [3] The active integration of citizen experiences as part of a larger research project is widely used in several aligned policy-based disciplines. For example, environmental scientists call it "citizen science" that entails citizen volunteers uploading observed ecosystem data; community health investigators recognize it as being part of Community-Based Participatory Research (CBPR) approach and integrate community partners throughout the entire research process which includes obtaining "insider" community experiences; and GIS cartographers call it Public Participation GIS (PPGIS) or Volunteered Geographic Information (VGI) and is when persons upload information (view of building) from their physical location.

Third, the community aspect inherent in qualitative research methods (Chapter 1) helps equalize the unequal power relationship between the planner and the community and this is part of the intent of citizen participation. Qualitative research requires the planner to interact with the community and go where they live and work and see what members of the community see and document what they experience. By the planner going out and learning from the community, she is able to generate community-grounded observations that give an active voice and generate images based on the community's lived experiences. As one focus group participant once told me in the middle of a meeting: "make sure you get all of this down, because this is how it is." It is the redistribution of research power that enables the community to have an active presence in planning and public policy research conclusions where the community's lived experiences have a direct contribution to the decision-making process that impacts their future.

WHEN DO PLANNERS AND POLICY MAKERS APPLY QUALITATIVE METHODS IN CITIZEN PARTICIPATION?

Planners seek community input when there are underrepresented groups of people with knowledge or lived experiences about situations that are not well understood by the researchers. [4] The "community's perspective" is a complex web of layered experiences with multiple takes on reality. Who planners identify as being part of the community is critically important because these persons represent the "community's perspective" in their citizen participation project. In general, planners are interested in obtaining one of two types of empirical community vistas in their community input investigations: "emic" and "etic" viewpoints. An "emic" community viewpoint is provided by community insiders whose everyday experience informs their understanding of what is going on within the community, while an "etic" community viewpoint provides an "objective" outsider perspective about what is happening with the community. Planners seek "insider" emic community observations when there is "informational uncertainty" on what is going on inside the community. [5] Planners seek "expert" etic community observations when they need larger "objective" observations by persons who work outside of the community and are able to provide a bigger-picture view of the community.

DOING QUALITATIVE CITIZEN PARTICIPATION RESEARCH

Three commonly applied qualitative techniques planners use to obtain community input are: walking interviews, stakeholder/key informant meetings, and Photovoice. Each approach has a distinct strength and weakness in terms of capturing emic and etic observations (see Table 7.1). Walking interviews and Photovoice are particularly good in capturing individualized emic observations from the community which translate to more equalization of power relations between the planner and the community. In exchange for being adept at capturing emic community observations, walking interviews and Photovoice require much smaller sampled populations (25 to 50 persons) in comparison to stakeholder/key informant investigations that can easily and quickly accommodate 100+ persons in a few short meetings. However, walking interviews are much more obtrusive than Photovoice, with the planner actively interacting with the people in the community, while in Photovoice the community works independently from the planner to generate their community observations. At the other end of the spectrum stakeholder/key

Table 7.1 Applying Qualitative Techniques in Citizen Participation

Qualitative Research Technique	Type of Data	Sample Size	Obtrusiveness	Emic or Etic	Level of Equalization of Power Relations
Walking Interviews	Detailed word accounts per interview	Very small, no more than 25	High	Mostly emic with some etic observations	High to moderate
Stakeholder Analysis/Key Informant Investigation	Short accounts	Very large (up to 100+) to very small (less than 5)	High to moderate	Mostly etic with some emic observations	Moderate to very low
Photovoice	Images with short accounts	Small, no more then 50	Very low	Only emic	Very high

informant investigations are particularly good at generating a wide range of emic and some etic observations, but are limited in transferring any research power to the community.

WALKING INTERVIEWS

The "walking interview" (also called "go-along interviews") is when the planner talks with a community member while receiving a "tour" of their neighborhood or other local context. Walking interviews are inherently situational (in situ) in that the planner has casual conversations with participants in their everyday contexts. [6] One strength to walking interviews is that the participant serves as a "tour guide" that significantly reduces the "typical power dynamic that exist between the interviewer and interviewee (as subject)". [7] Walking interviews allow members of the community to provide emic observations on what they experience living in the community and frame the conversation on what is relevant in their immediate environment.

Setting Up

The set-up for a walking interview study is a cross between a site reconnaissance investigation and structured/unstructured interviews. As an interview investigation, you first need to have a clear identification of which community perspective you are seeking and how it will contribute to the citizen participation project. Different subsections in the community have different experiences of the same places in their shared community space. For example, a real estate developer walking through a newly gentrifying community will see economic development potential while a long-time resident will see the evaporation of a well-established vibrant community. Per a site reconnaissance investigation, you need to establish your travel logistics to figure out what you will be seeing/sharing during your tour. The location of the walking tour and the general route you will be taking with your community guide needs to be framed by the purpose of the citizen input project. As common sense as it sounds, if you are generating community input on affordable housing, your walking interviews should be in residential neighborhoods.

After figuring who you are walking with, how their experiences connect to the citizen participation project, and roughly what location you will be touring, you next need to do some homework before you go on your walking interviews. It is common practice for the researcher to visit the community ahead of time to get a sense of the walking tour context. Also, getting preliminary information about the immediate area (location on a map, history, census statistics) will allow you to ask more informed questions during the tour.

Getting the Data

There are several ways you can record your walking interview data and you are actively encouraged to record photographic data during your tour. Verbal data are most important in your walking interview as part of your community input project. There are a few ways you can capture verbal data during your walk. First, you need to record what was said in the walking interview. Bring a handy note pad and pen (or use the text app on your cellphone or tablet) and record on the spot comments made by your community tour guide. Your community tour guide will be providing lots of geo-specific comments and you need to capture as verbatim as possible what they said and where. You may want to record the interviews, but be cautious here. In the end, the strategy of recording you use for your walking interviews "depends on the variable comfort level of informants" as well as your personal preferences as a researcher. [8] Second, use your cellphone to take quick pictures along the walk to capture the physical cues that sparked the particularly insightful comments during the tour. Lastly, you need to record the entire event in a walking tour interview field journal. Each walking tour needs to be recorded and documented—community tour guide name and brief biography, day and time of the walk, tour route, and critical highlights of the interview. In addition, as you would in your field notes journal (Chapter 2), it is important to quickly record what was said immediately after the walking interview so you can best capture what your community tour guide shared during the walk.

Some community researchers integrate more sophisticated technologies in their walking interviews. For example, Carpiano in his walking interviews in Harmony Heights brought a cassette recorder with a lapel clip microphone and audio-recorded all his walking interviews. [9] Evans and Jones in their Rescue Geography project, integrated Global Positioning System (GPS) technology with GIS and audio recordings during their walking interviews to provide a spatial transcript of their walking interviews. [10]

ORGANIZING THE DATA

The foundation to your walking interview data is the geo-reference discussions you have with your community tour guide. During the walking interview, the community member you are interviewing will make vague references to the immediate environment ("Those houses over there …"). Make sure you either record comments with specific locational references in your note pad (cellphone, tablet) or take an image with your cellphone and provide a contextual text to the image. [11] If you do not audio record your interview, you will need to write up your conversation in your walking interview journal. The walking interview journal can be organized according to the Shatzman and Strauss field notes model (Chapter 2) with your interview data recorded in the Observational Notes section.

If you decide to take photographic images during the walking interview, integrate them in your walking interview journal. Fortunately, unlike in a photographic investigation that can total several dozens of images in a single outing, you will only take a handful of images in each walking interview. Copy and paste all of the quotes from the interview section that was prompted by or has some reference to the object in the image. Be open to the possibility of connecting an image from one part of the interview tour (abandoned house) to other sections of the interview that rediscusses an earlier observation.

Analyzing the Data

A unique characteristic to walking interviews is the multitude of data points that are analyzed by the planner. You will be analyzing verbal comments embedded in a moving geography that are interlaced with photographic documentation. Walking interviews require the integration of three types of qualitative analyses: content analysis for the verbal data; site reconnaissance analysis of the unfolding geography; and photographic analysis of the images taken along the walk. The content analysis of your walking interviews will largely be guided by the questions in the interview guide. Here, you will organize the relevant comments made during the walking tours along each interview guide question. At the same time, you need to be flexible for unanticipated insights shared during the tours and analyze them in a topical "etc." section in your analysis. If you are able to record photographic images during the work, you will need to embed the images within your analysis of the verbal data.

The site reconnaissance analysis of your walking tour observations is what was said during the walk geo-referenced to places along the tour route (street intersection, park, rail road tracks, etc.). Again, carefully documenting your tour route is very important because the path you take during your walking interview will significantly influence the perspective of what is mentioned during the interview. Lastly, the photographic analysis will be very straightforward and is basically you documenting important geo-referenced points made by the community member during the tour. Let the words of your community tour guide do the work in explaining why the images are significant to the citizen participation project.

Margaret Kusenbach provides an extensive overview on the types of observations community members make during their walking interviews. [12] She identifies five thematic types of comments: (1) *perception* (i.e. how the informant sees their environment based on their practical day-to-day knowledge); (2) *spatial practices* (i.e. ways in which people interact with their environment—walking their dog, taking out the trash, etc.); (3) *biographies* (i.e. the environment people occupy on a daily basis and how space becomes a catchment to their lived experiences—they found a dog here last year); (4) *social architecture* (i.e. the relationships between people in a spatial context); and, (5) *social realms* (i.e. how people act and social norms they share with local members in the community). [13]

STAKEHOLDER ANALYSIS/KEY INFORMANT INVESTIGATIONS

Stakeholder Analysis (SA) is a cross-sectional approach to analyzing several communities ("stakeholders") who have a stake in a particular plan or policy proposal. Unlike traditional qualitative research strategies that strive to isolate a specific community experience in their investigation, a planner takes to a SA because it allows her to holistically look at her community and integrate multiple and many times contradictory community experiences in the analysis of the community's perspective. Stakeholder investigations can include a large sample of the community (n=100+) when the planner takes a large-scale perspective on everyone impacted by a proposed project. SA is widely used on an international scale and has become an extremely popular approach used in environmental and community health planning over the last 10 years.

In contrast, key informant investigations are when the planner purposefully seeks out a specific grouping of individuals whose professional and/or organizational roles represent important technical expertise or specialized knowledge that is understood as being relevant to a planning outcome. [14] Key informants are chosen based on their "particular areas of expertise" and are easily accessible to the planner. [15] Key informant investigations can be based on a very small sample of the population when the planner is facing a very technically complicated problem and/or access to "known" experts/representatives is limited as a function of distance and availability.

Setting Up

The most important step in conducting a stakeholder analysis is determining "who are the stakeholders?" The underlying assumption in the identification of stakeholders is that they "have valuable knowledge and resources to contribute to plan development." [16] Unfortunately, there is no systematic approach on

how you should select your stakeholders. This is a function of the citizen participation process that is accessing SA as part of a one-of-a-kind planning project.
Focus on the planning project objectives and the larger policy context to help
guide you in the development of your criteria in the selection of stakeholders.
A variety of selection criteria variables have been identified in the stakeholder
analysis literature and includes: [17]

- Geographic proximity
- Interest in the project
- Institution
- Political influence
- Access to resources
- Potential conflicts and coalitions between stakeholders.

Selecting key informants is a bit more straightforward in comparison to the
stakeholder analysis. Here, you are looking for individuals that meet at least two
criteria. First, you are looking for individuals who have "expert" knowledge on
a topic that you know very little about that is relevant to the planning issue at
hand. In your search for experts, make sure you secure individuals who are not
only knowledgeable about your topic, but are willing to share their information
and are able to educate you about the multiple perspectives on your topic. Second,
you want to find key informants who perform valuable "gatekeeper" access to
the community or environs that you need to access for your planning investigation. Key informant researchers are clear in discouraging you from recruiting
local knowledgeable residents as key informants. Community members belong
in a stakeholder analysis. Gatekeepers in a key informant investigation are those
persons who

> represent a specialized segments [sic] of the community and although
> they may official [sic] speak for community members, their perspectives
> or opinions are again not necessarily representative and they may not be
> in a position to facilitate access to a sufficiently diverse or representative
> segment of the community. [18]

Getting the Data

Several qualitative research techniques can be used in a stakeholder analysis. The
degree of community involvement is a critical point in SA because it influences
the entire citizen participation process, in particular the choice of participation

technique. [19] Citizen participation processes that are more integrative and strive to equalize power relations between the community and planner operationally will require several meetings throughout the planning process and provide a qualitative platform that allows the community to have control over the narrative in meetings. Here, focus group-style stakeholder meetings, field interviews, or community workshops are examples of collaborative participatory qualitative techniques. In contrast, qualitative techniques that require little to no communication between the community and the planner (newsletters, reports, or webpages) or only result in a single meeting with the community (townhall meeting) serve an informational function for the planner and do little in equalizing power relations with the community.

The planner is very focused on getting the correct phrasing from their informants when conducting a key informant investigation and will apply qualitative techniques that allow for careful recording of what was said as well as provide opportunities for the planner to ask follow-up questions. The planner will usually apply a semi-structured interview strategy when the number of key informants in the citizen participation projects is smaller (± 20) and that the area of sought-after expertise is very narrow with only a small number of accessible experts. In addition, the planner is motivated to apply an interview key informant investigation if some of the needed information is either private, confidential, or if the key informant (especially "gatekeeper" informants) cannot publicly be seen collaborating with the planner. For larger key informant projects (20+) where the range of "expertise" is broadly defined and the access to key informants is logistically difficult for the planner to manage, she will implement a survey that will include open-ended and closed questions.

Organizing the Data

It is very important that you document who said what in both your stakeholder and key informant meetings. Both citizen participation techniques are singularly premised on a purposeful sampling strategy where you directly access the primary source of community information with the intent of capturing the "community's voice." It is for this reason that a one-time large stakeholder meeting where it is not possible to isolate who said what during the session is a form of SA that is "an empty and frustrating process for the powerless." [20] The planner can only clump all of the comments into one "community perspective" although several different emic and etic positions may have been discussed in the meeting.

At the completion of your SA and key informant investigation you will end up with a cache of raw interview transcript files. You will sequentially organize your data in two ways. First, with your interview guide serving as a template, copy and paste all of the comments for each question from your interview transcript file and list them per question with their stakeholder/key informant identification (e.g. store owner, local resident, hydrologist, etc.). This will allow you to generate a breadth of observations per interview question. Next, create a new file and organize your stakeholder/key informant responses into "shared observations" and "other" according to the interview guide question. This second organization of community comments into categories of "shared observations" and "other" will highlight the coalescence/non-coalescences of different perspectives in relation to your interview guide question.

Analyzing the Data

You will analyze the stakeholder and key informant comments via a manifest content analysis and apply an identification/definition and pattern investigations. First, apply the identification/definition investigation to more closely examine how topics are defined per stakeholder/key informant perspective. Anticipate the possibility that stakeholders and key informants will define the same topic (neighborhood park) in very different ways. This is a good thing and is equal to the "thick description" internal validity criterion in qualitative research and is evidence that you have a multi-dimensional understanding of key topics in the community.

In your pattern investigation, pay extra attention to whether a community perspective profile emerges from the stakeholder/key informant comments. For example, is there a connection between the availability of sidewalks, adequacy of street lighting, and concerns about local crime that makes a particular neighborhood less walkable? In addition, your pattern investigation may highlight shared understandings among dissimilar community and expert perspectives. For example, shop owners, police officers, and local residents may all share the same understanding about the lack of walkability in a neighborhood from completely different experienced vistas.

PHOTOVOICE

Photovoice is a research technique that is actively used within the Participant Action Research (PAR) and Community-based Participatory Research (CBPR) research designs that focuses on empowering "marginalized" community residents in an effort to create positive change. [21] Photovoice is a research technique that provides community members with cameras to document what they experience in their day-to-day lives. Photovoice is a vivid way for community residents "to show firsthand their perceived strengths and needs, to promote critical dialogue and knowledge about their community assets and concerns, and to reach policymakers through images and stories of everyday life to bring about change". [22] Community residents providing their unique vista, with their shared images integrated with their own narrative in how these images are discussed, performs an equalizing power relation function: The community has more control in how its perspective is defined in the citizen participation process.

Setting Up

Photovoice is a very involved research process for both the planner and the community. More than half of the work that goes into conducting a Photovoice project is in the set-up stage. The research process is organized into four stages and is broken down into a nine-step process: [23]

I. **Set-up**: (1) Identification of Community Issue. Identify issues that are relevant to the larger goals of the citizen participation project. Community issues can be determined independently of the community or collaboratively between the planner and community leaders. (2) Participant Recruitment. Purposeful sampling strategy to identify local residents who can provide emic community insights.

II. **First Community Meeting**: (3) Photovoice Training. Train community residents on the Photovoice process and secure consent forms for their participation. (4) Camera Distribution and Instructions. Provide a brief overview about photographic research process and distribute cameras to community members. (5) Identification of Photo Assignment. This is where the planner connects the Identification of Community Issues to a shooting guide (Chapter 3) that identifies the location and primary variables that the community members need to capture with their cameras. (6) Photo Assignment Discussion. The planner introduces "trigger questions" ("what do you see in this image?" and "what is your explanation of what is happening in the image?" and "what can we do to fix this?") that will be used in the next meeting's discussion of images.

III. **Research and Analysis**: (7) Community Photographic Investigation. Community members go out into their community and take images of what they know based on the provided Photo Assignment. (8) Data Analysis and Final Report. The planner convenes a second meeting where community members present their images and the group discuss what everyone learned from each of the presentations. (Another option is to forgo the second community meeting and for the planner to simply conduct independent interviews with each community photographer.) After the second meeting, the planner organizes the community images and verbal conversations into a final report.

IV. **Connection to the Citizen Participation Process**: (9) Presentation of Photovoice Findings. Planner integrates the Photovoice project into the citizen participation process and presents the "community's perspective."

Getting the Data

Part of the empowering process in Photovoice is having trained community members generating photographic images of how they see their community for the citizen participation process. The verbal data generated during the community's discussion of their images are captured by the planners either through a group meeting or individual interviews. Here, planners need to pay attention to who took each image and document how the photographers described their images.

Organizing the Data

Photovoice produces three distinct data sets that requires careful tagging before you analyze them so as not to lose the connection of who said what per image. The data sets are (a) grouping of images captured per community member; (b) analysis of images generated by the community photographer; and (c) analysis of the images by other members of the community during the group discussion meeting. Knowing who took each image is very important in understanding the explanatory value of the image. Each shot is a reflection of the photographer's view of the research subject. A brief biography tag of each community member is needed so you know their individual characteristic (youth, disabled, over 65 years old, homeless, undocumented immigrant, long-time resident, etc.) as it relates to their analysis of images.

Make sure to separate the community photographer comments about their images from comments by other members of the community about the same set of images. Use the Identification of Photo Assignment (Step 5) provided to the community photographers before they went out to the field to organize the discussion by community members per set of images. It may be practical to limit the number of images each community member shares in the second group meeting to "top three images" to allow everyone in the group to share their images within a two-hour meeting. Keep track of the photographer's comments on their images in relation to other group members' comments on the same image. Connecting who said what per image may provide an added insight into how different members of the community have different understandings about shared community resources.

Analyzing the Data

Photovoice investigations require the planner to integrate two types of qualitative analyses: Content analysis and photographic analysis. The content analysis of verbal accounts will be organized around the Identification of Community Issues criteria and are differentiated between the community photographer's comments and community members' observations. Pay particular attention to how the community photographer defines key concepts, look for linkages between key concepts, and see if they provide any causal explanations on how changes in one variable (e.g. closing of a local factory) facilitated a change in another variable (increase in the number of abandoned homes). Accounts of how residents see things that are interrelated to each other provides the building blocks for developing planning recommendations from the community's perspective.

Two photographic analyses take place in a Photovoice investigation. The first set of analyses is conducted by the community photographer and the community members and is the emic accounts of how they understand each image in the study. The second analysis is conducted by the planner and is the collective assessment of all the images taken during the Photovoice investigation. Here, you have the unique opportunity to analyze possible patterns in how local residents see their community. For example, do several of the community participants take very similar images of the local park? Although Photovoice uses photographic images as empirical bits of evidence, it is important to keep in mind that they are data with a small "d" in comparison to the much more valued verbal qualitative transcript data with a big "D" generated by the community members. [24]

CASE STUDY #1 PHOTOVOICE: THE ROLE OF NEIGHBORHOOD PHYSICAL AND SOCIAL ENVIRONMENTS IN OLDER ADULTS' PHYSICAL ACTIVITY

Mahmood et al. provide one example in applying the Photovoice technique to better understand how the physical and social environments influence physical activity among older adults in Vancouver, British Columbia, Canada, and Greater

Portland, Oregon, USA. [25] The Photovoice project took a little over a year and was part of a larger three-year study that included 34 older adults from Vancouver, British Columbia, and 32 older adults from Greater Portland, all of whom were 65 years or over. Participants were asked by the researchers to go out into their neighborhoods and photograph perceived physical and social barriers to their physical activity. A key part in the recruitment of participants for the study, researchers made sure each participant was able to attend one catered half-day training session and one catered half-day discussion session. A participant package was handed out at the training session that included: a 27-exposure disposable camera, photo-journal to document where each picture was taken and the reason behind taking the picture, general information on the study and photography tips, picture-taking consent forms, a postage-paid envelope and instructions. [26]

Before attending the discussion session, participants were asked to pick six to eight images that best captured the issues they were trying to document in their photo-journal. The discussion session was divided into two smaller sessions. In the first session, participants were randomly divided into small groups where each participant shared their images with their group. All the participants came together as whole in the second session and critically discussed issues identified in the images. Seven major themes emerged from the images and corresponding descriptions and discussions: Being safe and feeling secure, getting there, comfort in movement, diversity of destinations, community-based programs, peer support, and intergenerational/volunteer activities. The Photovoice project allowed older adults to capture facilitators and barriers for physical activity in their social and physical environments through their own "lens", and the process of taking photographs, writing, and discussing their content provided a unique opportunity to reflect on the significance of neighborhood environment (physical and social) in fostering active aging. [27]

Safety and security was the most photographed and discussed theme in both Vancouver and Portland regions. A prominent mobility barrier for older adults was uneven sidewalks or damaged pavement, making it difficult for the participants to walk in their neighborhoods (see Figure 7.1). In one discussion session, one participant shared "[The streets near my home have] no sidewalks, no shoulders on one side, poor visibility due to curve. This is my only access to church and a bus stop ... I walk here but don't enjoy it." [28]

Figure 7.1 Sample Photographs and Quotes for "Being Safe and Feeling Secure"

DISCUSSION QUESTIONS

1. Why are qualitative research techniques relevant to the citizen participation process?
2. Some qualitative research techniques are particularly good at accessing hard-to-reach emic and etic community member perspectives. Outline a citizen participation proposal that combines two different qualitative research techniques (for example, Walking interviews and key informant analysis) to access one emic perspective and one etic perspective.
3. Selection bias is a very significant problem in all citizen participation projects. How can you guard against sampling bias in Walking interviews, Stakeholder Analysis, and Photovoice community research projects? It is possible or desirable to mitigate against sampling bias in any citizen participation project?

REFERENCES

[1] Arnstein, S. 1969. "A ladder of citizen participation," *Journal of American Institute of Planner*, 35(4), pp. 216–224, p. 216.
[2] Luyet, V., Schlaepfer, R., Parlange, M., and Buttler, A. 2012. "A framework to implement stakeholder participation in environmental projects", *Journal of Environmental Management*, 111, pp. 213–219, p. 214.
[3] Gaber and Overacker, 2015. p. 117, Dewey, J. 1905. "The realism of pragmatism," *Journal of Philosophy, Psychology & Scientific Methods*, 2, pp. 324–327, Dewey, J. 1969. "Psychology and philosophical method," *The Early Works of John Dewey, 1882–1898*, p. 1, Boydston,

JA. (ed), pp. 158-167, Schusterman, R. 1990. "Dewey on experience: Foundation or Reconstruction?" in *Dewey Reconfigured: Essays on Deweyian Pragmatism*, edited by Casey, H. and Seiple, D. New York: NY, State University of New York Press.

[4] Newig, J., Pahl-Wostl, C., and Sigel, K. 2005. "The role of public participation in managing uncertainty in the implementation of the water framework directive," *European Environment*, 15, pp. 333–343.

[5] Pike, K. 1990. *Emics and Etics: The insider/outsider debate*, Los Angeles, CA, Sage Publications. Pike, K. 1967. *Language n Relation to a Unified Theory of Structure of Human Behavior*, The Hague: Mouton and Co. Onwuegbuzie, A., and Johnson, B. 2008. "The validity issue in mixed research," in *The Mixed Methods Reader*, Clark, V., and Creswell, J. (eds). Los Angeles: CA, Sage Publications, pp. 271-298, 290.

[6] Kusenbach, M. 2003. "Street phenomenology: The go-along ethnographic research tool," *Ethnography*, 4(3), pp. 455–485.

[7] Carpiano, R. 2009. "Come take a walk with me: The 'Go-Along' interview as a novel method for studying the implications of place for health and well-being," *Health and Place*, 15, pp. 263–272, p. 264.

[8] Kusenbach, "Street phenomenology," p. 465.

[9] Carpiano, "Come take a walk".

[10] Evans, J., and Jones, P. 2011. "The walking interview: Methodology, mobility and place," *Applied Geography*, 31, pp. 849–858.

[11] Carpiano, "Come take a walk," p. 270.

[12] Kusenbach, "Street phenomenology."

[13] Amy, E., Mayer, J., Rafii, R., Housemann, R., Brownson, R., and King, A. 1999. "Key informant surveys as a tool to implement and evaluate physical activity interventions in the community," *Health Education Research*, 14(2), pp. 289–298.

[14] McKenna, S., Iwasaki, P., Stewart, T., and Main, D. 2011. "Key informants and community members in Community-Based Participatory Research: One is not like the other," *Progress in Community Health Partnerships: Research, Education, and Action*, 5(4), pp. 387–397, p. 388.

[15] Brody, S. 2003. "Measuring the effects of stakeholder participation on the quality of local plans based on the principles of collaborative ecosystem management," *Journal of Planning Education and Research*, 22, pp. 407–419, p. 410.

[16] Luyet et al., "Framework." Rauam, Susanne. 2018. "A framework for integrating systematic stakeholder analysis in ecosystem services research: Stakeholder mapping for forest ecosystem services in the UK," *Ecosystem Services*, 29, pp. 170–184.

[17] McKenna, S., and Main, D., 2013. "The role and influence of key informants in community-engaged research: A critical perspective," *Action Research*, 11(2), pp. 113–124, p. 117.

[18] Luyet et al., "Framework," p. 216.

[19] Arnstein, "Ladder," p. 216.

[20] Arnstein, "Ladder," p. 216.

[21] Wang, C., and Burris, M.A. 1997. "Photovoice: Concept, methodology, and use for participatory needs assessment," *Journal of Health Education and Behavior*, 24, pp. 369–387; Wang, Caroline., Wu, Yi., Zahn, Tao., and Carovano, K. (1998). "Photovoice as a participatory health promotion strategy," *Health Promotion International*, 13(1), pp. 75–86; Castleden, Heather, Garvin, Theresa, Huu-ay-aht, F. N. 2008. "Modifying Photovoice for community-based participatory Indigenous research, *Social Science and Medicine*, 66, pp. 1393–1405.

[22] Wang and Burris, "Photovoice," p. 382.

[23] Wang, C. 2006. "Youth participation in Photovoice as a strategy for community change," *Journal of Community Practice*, 14(1–2), pp. 147–161.

[24] Catalani, C., and Minkler, M. 2010. "Photovoice: A review of the literature in health and public health,"*Health Education Behavior*, 37(3), pp. 424–451.

[25] Mahmood, A., Chaudhury, H., Michael, Y., Campo, M., Hay, K., and Sarte, A. 2012. "A photovoice documentation of the role of neighborhood physical and social environments in older adults' physical activity in two metropolitan areas in North America," *Social Science and Medicine*, 74, pp. 1180–1192.

[26] Mahmood et al., "Photovoice documentation," p. 1181.

[27] Mahmood et al., "Photovoice documentation," p. 1190.

[28] Mahmood et al., "Photovoice documentation," p. 1183.

INDEX

CPSIA information can be obtained
at www.ICGtesting.com
Printed in the USA
LVHW080952011121
702107LV00012B/104